NEVER TRY TO TEACH
A PIG TO SING

Humor in Life and Letters Series

A complete listing of the books in this series can be found at the back of this volume.

ALAN DUNDES   CARL R. PAGTER

NEVER TRY TO TEACH A PIG TO SING

Still More Urban Folklore from the
Paperwork Empire

Wayne State University Press   Detroit

95   94   93   92   91   5   4   3   2   1

Library of Congress Cataloging-in-Publication Data
Dundes, Alan.
     Never try to teach a pig to sing : still more urban folklore from
the paperwork empire / Alan Dundes and Carl R. Pagter
          p.   cm. — (Humor in life and letters)
     ISBN 0-8143-2357-X (alk. paper) —
     ISBN 0-8143-2358-8 (pbk.: alk. paper)
     1. Urban folklore—United States. 2. Xerography—Folklore.
3. Office practice—United States—Folklore. 4. American wit and
humor. I. Pagter, Carl R., 1934-   . II. Series.
GR105.D85 1991
817'.54080321732—dc20   90-28451

Designer: Elizabeth Pilon

Contents

When Things Go Wrong   128

Quick on the Draw: Folk Cartoons   277

The Battle of the Sexes 344

Preface

This third collaboration between a professor of folklore and an attorney whose avocation is folksinging could not have occurred without the generous assistance of students, colleagues, friends, and readers of the previous two volumes who were kind enough to share unsolicited exemplars of office-copier folklore with us. Our own collections spanning some twenty-five years made it obvious that this stream of urban folklore has continued to be a lively and prolific one. Even this volume does not begin to exhaust the richness of the folklore transmitted by copier machine.

We wish to express out sincerest gratitude to all of the following contributors whose materials we have included and apologize to any whose names we may have inadvertently omitted. George W. Adams, Kingsley Anderson, Karol Andrews, Bob Armstrong, J. T. Ball, Judith Barnes, Alison Becker, Susan Bennett, Chick Berkstresser, Kathleen R. Bomba, Patti Breitman, David Broome, Carla Jean Bundrick, Susan Carlson, Juliet Carrara, V. Cespedes, John Cherry, Lee Chic, George Coe, Emily Copenhauer, Margaret Daly, Helen Dampsey, Michael Davison, Trudy De Leon, Diana De Truree, Mandalit Del Barco, Don Denison, Stacy H. Dobrzensky, James Drahos, Becky Epperson, Judy Evans, Will Evans, Debra Farrington, Elizabeth Fassett, Allene Fernandez, Jill Foley, Derek Frowne, Kim Futerman, Victoria George, Shirley Gillim, Gina Giumarra, Gwendolyn Glerum, James Goulet, Diane Green, Donna Gregg, Catherine Griffin, Thomas D. Hall, Stuart Hay, George Hempstead, Marin Higgins, Bill Holt, Doug Howard, David Hunn, Tom Hunt, Sondra Jarvis, Betty Johnson, Steve Kassovic, Carolyn Keith, Barbara Kirshenblatt-Gimblett, Mary Koske, D. Lee Kvalnes, Michael Larson, W. J. Lindgren, Kim McCloud, Pete McCorkell, Bonnie Messenger, Frank Miller, Larry Miller, Margo Miller, Michael E. Miller, Lonnie Moore, John Morgan, Bob Murphy, Shirley Nowicki, Tom

O'Connor, Kathy Odean, Eileen O'Hara, Marilyn Owen, Cheryl Pagter, Edward S. Pagter, Barbara Papini, Kirk Pfaffenberger, Margot M. Ray, L. A. Rebhun, Charles W. Reese, Alison Dundes Renteln, Rosalind Ribnick, Nancy Ridenour, Lars Rohrbach, Shirley Rothstein, Edith T. Rowe, Nick Royal, Michael Ruggiero, John Sandy, Ted Schucat, Jim Seymour, Esther Shimizu, Curtis Shirley, Betty Silva, David Silverman, Cheryl Simmons, Jim Simpson, Perry Simpson, Natalie Skeels, John Snodgrass, Emily Socolov, Dave Strang, Louise Suarez, Carolyn Tauxe, Donald W. Te Brest, Ruth Thompson, Marie Thornton, Lena Ting, Mary Tromp, Kathy Tyler, Robert L. White, Patricia McQuoun Wildermuth, Sue Williams, Monique Young, and Maury P. Zapata.

We are especially indebted to Carol Bird, Simon J. Carmel, Craig Kilpatrick, Lorne Mellors, the late Peter Tamony, and Edward Willer who sent us substantial numbers of office folklore exemplars from their own personal collections.

By far the vast majority of urban folklore is anonymous and bears no marks of attribution. In some instances, we suspect that a given item may have originated with a professional writer or cartoonist. In the few cases where attributions are given, we have included them, even though the alleged author or cartoonist may in fact not have been the original source of the items, but merely the local transmitter of a particular version. The very process of folklore transmission from person to person generally tends to eliminate the names of original composers. One must also keep in mind that professional writers and cartoonists occasionally borrow materials from the anonymous folk tradition. In such a situation, the presence of a name on an item may disguise its folk origin. If in fact there is unattributed copyrighted material included in this volume, it is because the name of the author has disappeared in the folk transmission process.

Introduction

When we first published *Urban Folklore from the Paperwork Empire* in 1975 (later reissued as *Work Hard and You Shall Be Rewarded* in paperback in 1978), we did not fully realize the enormity of the tradition we had sampled. In retrospect, we can see that the one hundred or so items we initially reported were but the tip of the iceberg. In our second volume, *When You're Up to Your Ass in Alligators . . .*, published in 1987, we included an additional one hundred and forty illustrations of the urban folklore transmitted by office copier machines. These two previous compilations provided some idea of the richness and diversity of this tradition, but by no means did they exhaust the material available in active circulation. Moreover, brand new exemplars continued to appear. The present volume contains specimens of older items which have been passed on for decades as well as relatively newly created office folklore.

We are pleased to observe that our earlier prediction that office copier folklore was bound to occur in other countries, especially those in which photocopier or facsimile machines abound, proved to be accurate. Published collections of office copier folklore from Denmark, England, Germany, and Sweden attest to the international distribution of many individual items. Just as folktales and folksongs enjoy cross-cultural provenance, so also does office copier folklore. The vexing question of what to call these materials is still not completely resolved. One English collection labels them "Office Graffiti" while a Danish compilation proposes "Kopifitti." In any event, the speed and ease of dissemination of office copier folklore is surely a tribute to the effectiveness of modern communications technology. We anticipate that the distribution of office copier folklore will continue to expand, and we will not be surprised to see parallel collections published in other industrial societies.

The eventual publication of office copier folklore elsewhere in the world will one day facilitate fascinating comparative studies as each country and culture adapts these remarkable traditions to fit its own worldview.

Even in the relatively few collections of office copier folklore published thus far, we have noticed cultural differences in terms of what can or cannot be published. For example, there are at least sixty or seventy items in active circulation in the United States which by American standards would be deemed obscene. These materials are blatantly racist and sexist and in some cases are extremely crude, bordering on the pornographic. We have reluctantly excluded most of these items because otherwise we would not have been able to publish our collections with university or commercial presses. As it was, we encountered great difficulty in publishing our earlier anthologies. The first, written in 1970, was not published until 1975; the second, written before 1978, was not published until 1987. In the case of the first collection, the University of Texas Press, which produced the book, declined to put its imprimatur on the volume. Thus *Urban Folklore from the Paperwork Empire*, published in a brown paper jacket, bore only a box number in Austin, Texas, in lieu of the name of the University of Texas Press. Fortunately, the American Folklore Society understood the value of these folklore materials and had the courage to publish our first book even without a university press imprimatur. We were interested to see that the Danish, German, and Swedish collections were able to include some of the more arguably obscene exemplars. We look forward to a time in the United States when scholars will be free to publish all the folklore they collect and will no longer be subject to censorship by a university press or forced to indulge in self-censorship. The curious irony is that these supposed "obscene" materials circulate freely among some of the folk, but nevertheless cannot be included in this volume. This situation is in fact an important commentary on the very nature of folklore. Often folklore contains content of a salacious or "offensive" nature. The translation of folklore material into a written academic format is difficult. In the same way there are plenty of traditional oral jokes which cannot be told on commercial radio stations or published in family newspapers. Some of the office copier traditions fall into that category.

In general, we have continued to abide by the definitional criteria for folklore of multiple existence and variation. By multiple existence, we mean that an item must exist in more than one

place and/or time. In other words, there must be at least two versions of any item in order for it to qualify as bona fide folklore,
and there must also be variation. It is the variation in fact which
confirms the folk process at work. Each link in the chain of transmission has the possibility of altering or "improving" the item in
some way. While one might logically assume that the use of the
photo-copier would guarantee the exact replication of each item,
the overwhelming evidence is to the contrary. No two versions of
an item of office copier folklore will be precisely identical. This
has remained true even with the advent of the telecopier or tele-
fax—shorthand for telephone facsimile. We have made a conscious
effort to include several versions of items in this compilation to
demonstrate the subtle nature of such variation.

It would not be practical in an anthology of this kind for us
to present all the versions of the items we have included. In some
cases, we have more than fifteen different versions of one item.
Often, it was hard for us to select the one or two illustrations to
represent the item in the volume. In future research, it would surely
be of interest to include a truly comprehensive set of illustrations
of a given item.

The titles of our items are usually taken from the items themselves. Where there was no title given, we have endeavored to
choose a title from within the text. Wherever possible, we have provided annotation, referring to the same or related items in other
compilations.

We have somewhat arbitrarily divided our corpus into seven
chapters. Our classification is not intended to be a hard and fast
one, but simply a convenient means of presenting our data in an
orderly fashion. We begin with "A Word to the Wise." This section
gives would-be explanations of words, phrases, and terminology.
The second chapter, "Signs of the Times," is very much centered
in the context of an office where one might see such items on
bulletin boards or affixed to a wall or attached to a coffee dispenser
or occasionally on the copy machine itself. Chapter three continues the theme of office life, but concentrates on disasters in
the workplace. We have entitled it "When Things Go Wrong." The
fourth chapter, "From Bad to Verse" samples some of the folk poetry
in circulation. The fifth chapter "Different Strokes for Different
Folks" focuses on group and individual differences, including ethnic
slurs. Chapter six, "Quick on the Draw: Folk Cartoons," contains
folk cartoons, a sub-genre of office copier folklore sampled in the
earlier two collections. The seventh and final chapter is once again

thematic. Entitled "The Battle of the Sexes," it deals with gender stereotypes.

It is not always possible to estimate the age of individual items. Some clearly predate the office copier. This can be inferred from the content of items or occasionally verified by the existence of typewritten or dittoed or mimeographed or even printed versions. One must keep in mind that folklorists did not always make a point of collecting these items, preferring instead to concentrate on purely orally transmitted forms. There was also some prejudice against collecting modern or current folklore, which was thought to be ephemeral and insignificant, not worthy of serious consideration by scholars. Our point is that no folklore is insignificant or unworthy of critical scrutiny.

The popularity of some of the items is attested by their reproduction in mass or popular cultural form. One can find plaques, cards, certificates, or bumper stickers in novelty or gift shops which feature some of the office copier folklore. This reminds us of the inevitable interplay between folklore and mass culture. While the mass cultural renderings of the items might tend to favor one version over another, it seems unlikely that mass culture is the source of the folklore. Our data suggests that folklore comes first and then some enterprising entrepreneur puts the folklore on a plaque or card.

One thing this volume clearly demonstrates is the existence of folklore in the modern urban technological world. The idea that folklore reflects only the past is incorrect. Yes, some folklore reflects the past, but there is also folklore, ongoing, current, which reflects the present, the culture of today. As more and more individuals move from rural to urban settings, a trend which is observable in many parts of the world, the folklore of offices and of bureaucracy is bound to continue. The office copier greatly facilitates the transmission of this folklore. For this reason, we think it is incumbent upon folklorists to document this tradition, and to document it as it happens. Were folklorists to wait fifty or one hundred years to investigate the traditions contained in this book, they might be unable to do so. Not many libraries or archives make a point of collecting such materials. Familiar as many of these items will surely be to individual readers, one may legitimately raise the question of where would or could an individual put his or her hands on illustrations of these items. After a time, they tend to disappear from the office bulletin board or they are passed on by individuals who fail to retain a copy. Fortunately, there are collectors and devotees of these fascinating materials, some of whom have been willing to share their collections with us.

Finally, we want to remind our readers that we have made a conscious effort to present the materials as we received them. We have resisted the temptation to re-draw the cartoons or to "correct" typographical or grammatical errors in the texts. Were we to do so, we would have reduced the value of this folklore. The folk cartoons, for example, are *not* drawn by the sorts of professional cartoonists whose work may be found in *Esquire, Punch,* the *New Yorker, Playboy,* and newspapers. Rather they are drawn by ordinary people who may or may not possess great artistic talent. Such materials are presented here not necessarily for their aesthetic appeal but for purposes of demonstrating the nature of a particular traditional item.

We continue to marvel at the variety and creativity of the folk expressions sampled in this volume. The folk seem to have an unending supply of urban folklore from the paperwork empire. We hope that readers will come to share our delight in these imaginative and revealing materials.

Abbreviations

Wherever possible, we have tried to locate parallel cognate versions of the items included in this volume. Because there are still relatively few major collections of folklore transmitted by office copier machines, we have elected to list these collections here. Since we cite some of these sources throughout our volume, we have used the following abbreviations:

CS   Else Marie Kofod, *Chefens Sekretaer Og andre beske kommentarer til hverdagens fortraedeligheder* (Aalborg: Det Schonbergske Forlag, 1988)

IK   Uli Kutter, *Ich Kundige!!! Zeugnisse von Wünschen und Ängsten am Arbeitsplatz—Eine Bestandsaufnahme* (Marburg: Jonas Verlag, 1982)

ISR   Institute for Sex Research, 416 Morrison Hall, Indiana University, Bloomington, Indiana 47401

MF   Ulf Palmenfelt, *Modern Folkhumor: Folkhumor i fotostat* (Stockholm: Bokförlaget Prisma, 1986)

NLM   G. Legman, *No Laughing Matter: Rationale of the Dirty Joke—An Analysis of Sexual Humor*, Second Series (New York: Breaking Point, 1975)

OG2   Nicolas Locke, *Office Graffiti 2* (London: Proteus Books, 1981)

OHB   Pete Fagan and Mark Schaffer, *The Office Humour Book* (London: Angus & Robertson, 1986)

RDJ	G. Legman, *Rationale of the Dirty Joke—An Analysis of Sexual Humor* First Series (New York: Grove Press, 1968)
RIF	Paul Smith, *Reproduction Is Fun* (London: Routledge & Kegan Paul, 1986)
RJ	Anon., *Rugby Jokes in the Office* (London: Sphere Books, 1989)
TCB	Paul Smith, *The Complete Book of Office Mis-Practice* (London: Routledge & Kegan Paul, 1984)
UFFC-PC	Louis Michael Bell, Cathy Makin Orr, and Michael James Preston, *Urban Folklore from Colorado: Photocopy Cartoons* (Ann Arbor: Xerox University Microfilms, 1976)
UFFC-TB	Cathy Makin Orr and Michael James Preston, *Urban Folklore from Colorado: Typescript Broadsides* (Ann Arbor: Xerox University Microfilms, 1976)
WH	Alan Dundes and Carl R. Pagter, *Work Hard and You Shall Be Rewarded: Urban Folklore from the Paperwork Empire* (Bloomington: Indiana University Press, 1978)
WY	Alan Dundes and Carl R. Pagter, *When You're Up to Your Ass in Alligators . . . : More Urban Folklore from the Paperwork Empire* (Detroit: Wayne State University Press, 1987)
YD	Wayne B. Norris, *You Don't Have to Be Crazy to Work Here . . . But It Sure Helps* (Los Angeles: Price/Stern/Sloan, 1986)
YWIW	Nicolas Locke, *You Want It When?!! The Complete Office Graffiti* (London: Proteus Books, 1979)

A Word to the Wise

Folk speech is part of folklore. Each folk group has its own unique argot. Sometimes the esoteric or seemingly arcane nature of a group's folk speech causes amusement to outsiders. Explaining or defining common or uncommon terms of reference, peculiar to a given group, is a standard practice.

In this opening chapter containing folk definitions, we have included not only pseudo-attempts to explicate specialized vocabularies, but also efforts to define individual words or concepts. Under the rubric of "wise words," we have taken liberty of presenting discussions of names, recipes, and other verbal formulas. Almost all of the items contained in this chapter feature some form of wordplay.

1. Medical Terminology for the Layman

The medical profession has always had an aura of mystery. Its specialized vocabulary, often employing a combination of Latin terms and technical jargon, may bewilder the anxious patient. Not all doctors take the trouble to translate their diagnoses and prescriptions into terms the layman can understand. The following item, collected in Fishersville, Virginia, in 1989, pretends to demystify medical lingo.

MEDICAL TERMINOLOGY For The Layman:

ARTERY --	*The Study of fine paintings.*
BARIUM --	*What to do when CPR fails.*
CAESAREAN SECTION --	*A district in Rome.*
COLIC --	*A sheep-dog.*
COMA --	*A punctuation mark.*
CONGENITAL --	*Friendly.*
DILATE --	*To live longer.*
FESTER --	*Quicker.*
G.I. SERIES --	*Baseball series between teams of soldiers.*
GRIPPE --	*A suitcase.*
HANG-NAIL --	*A coat-hook.*
MEDICAL STAFF --	*A doctor's cane.*
MINOR OPERATION --	*Coal digging.*
MORBID --	*A higher offer.*
NITRATE --	*Lower than the day rate.*
NODE --	*Was aware of.*
ORGANIC --	*Musical.*
OUTPATIENT --	*A person who has fainted.*
POST-OPERATIVE --	*A letter carrier.*
PROTEIN --	*In favor of young people.*
SECRETION --	*Hiding anything.*
SEROLOGY --	*Study of English Knighthood.*
TABLET --	*A small table.*
TUMOR --	*An extra pair.*
URINE --	*Opposite of "You're out."*
VARICOSE VEINS --	*Veins which are very close together.*

2. The Electrocardial Guide

One area of medicine which is particularly anxiety-producing for the general public is cardiology. Fear of heart attack is widespread in the population. One of the technical innovations in the detection of heart disease is the electrocardiagraph, a galvanometric device that records heart activity. The resulting electrocardiagram is a graphic presentation useful in the prevention and diagnosis of heart disease. Most Americans are generally familiar with the graphic displays of heart activity if from no other source than from television shows ostensibly concerned with emergency room or intensive care procedures. Deciphering the electrocardiagram requires medical expertise on the part of a doctor or a trained technician.

The following item is a folk interpretation of the mysterious squiggles of the electrocardiagram. It was collected from the nurses' station of the Cardiac Intensive Care Unit at Presbyterian Hospital in San Francisco in 1979. The place of collection suggests that this may be an in-group piece of folklore designed to relieve the anxiety of working in such a stressful location as an intensive care unit. Not all the terms are in fact intelligible to the layman. For example, the mention of Wenkeback syndrome refers to Karel Frederik Wenckebach (1864–1940), a Dutch internist in Vienna, whose name has been given to a particular heart irregularity.

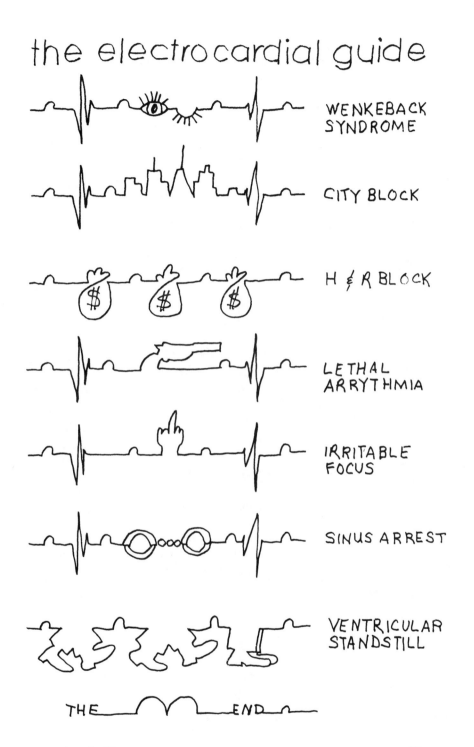

the electrocardial guide

WENKEBACK SYNDROME

CITY BLOCK

H & R BLOCK

LETHAL ARRYTHMIA

IRRITABLE FOCUS

SINUS ARREST

VENTRICULAR STANDSTILL

THE END

3. Employee Evaluation Form

Part of the promotion process depends upon employee performance ratings. Traditionally, employees never saw these evaluations and they could only guess at their content. However, federal legislation in the 1970s made it possible for employees to have access to their own personnel files. As a result, some business firms have instituted procedures whereby employees are shown the evaluation reports and asked to sign them, indicating that they have seen them. Consequently, some evaluators are reluctant to speak candidly, especially about poor performance on the job. The following item collected in Fishersville, Virginia, in 1989, is a pungent parody of the tendency to euphemize the terms of employee competence.

EMPLOYEE EVALUATION FORM

Under the FREEDOM of Information Act of 1974 and the Federal Privacy Act of 1976, I understand that my work performance is being documented. I have the right to examine and copy documentation. I have the right to review differences in order to resolve them, and I have the right to request amendments to and/or modification of any document.

NAME: _____   DATE: _____

KNOWLEDGE:	__	The son of a bitch really knows his shit
	__	Knows just enough to be dangerous
	__	Only half a brain and IS dangerous
	__	Fucking brain damaged. His coffee cup has a higher I.Q.
ACCURACY:	__	Does excellent work if not preoccupied with SEX
	__	Pretty Good; only occasionally blows it out his ass
	__	Has to take off his shoes to count higher than ten
	__	Couldn't count his balls and get the same number twice

ATTITUDE:	__	Extremely cooperative (if you kiss his ass frequently)
	__	Brown noser in good condition
	__	Often pisses off coworkers; thinks it's HIS section
	__	Doesn't give a shit, never did, never will
RELIABILITY:	__	Real dependable little cock sucker
	__	Can rely on him at evaluation time
	__	Can rely on him to be the first one out the fucking door
	__	Totally fucking worthless
APPEARANCE:	__	Extremely neat; even combs his pubic hair
	__	Looks great at evaluation time
	__	Dirty, filthy, smelly son of a bitch
	__	Flies leave fresh dog shit to follow him
PERFORMANCE:	__	Goes like a son of a bitch if there's money in it for him
	__	Does all kinds of good shit at evaluation time
	__	Works only if kicked in the ass every two minutes
	__	Couldn't do less work if he were in a fucking coma
LEADERSHIP:	__	Carries a chain saw and gets good results
	__	Better leader than fucking MacArthur at evaluation time
	__	Occasionally gets told to get fucked
	__	Mother Theresa told him to get fucked

I understand that I have been counseled and know my rights under the Privacy Act of 1988. I further acknowledge that "I am as fucked up as a football bat and will arrange to correct my deficiencies."

_____

signature

4. Terms Used in Writing Fitness Reports

As was noted in the previous item, there is a science, or perhaps it is an art, of writing letters of recommendation and filling out personnel evaluation forms. Again, most members of an in-group are well aware of the discrepancy between the terms used in official reports and the actual performance of the individuals being evaluated. Inflation occurs as often in the language of evaluation as it does in the economy. The bankruptcy of superlatives typically results in high-flown phrases of praise referring to mediocre if not substandard performance. The following guide for fitness report writers was collected at the Naval Air Station in Alameda, California, in the mid-1970s. Fitness reports are required for all U.S. military officers, and they play an important role with respect to whether or not a particular officer is promoted to a higher rank. Other versions of this item from the 1980s do not include a military frame of reference.

TERMS USED IN WRITING FITNESS REPORTS	DEFINITIONS
AVERAGE OFFICER	NOT TOO BRIGHT
EXCEPTIONALLY WELL QUALIFIED	HAS COMMITTED NO MAJOR BLUNDERS TO DATE
ACTIVE SOCIALLY	DRINKS HEAVILY
WIFE IS ACTIVE SOCIALLY	SHE DRINKS TOO
CHARACTER AND INTEGRITY ABOVE REPROACH	STILL ONE STEP AHEAD OF THE LAW
ZEALOUS ATTITUDE	OPINIONATED
EAGER TO FLY	TIME HOG
UNLIMITED POTENTIAL	WILL RETIRE AS COMMANDER
QUICK THINKING	OFFERS PLAUSIBLE EXCUSES FOR ERRORS
EXCEPTIONAL FLYING ABILITY	HAS AN EQUAL AMOUNT OF TAKEOFFS AND LANDINGS
TAKES PRIDE IN HIS WORK	CONCEITED
TAKES ADVANTAGE OF EVERY OPPORTUNITY TO PROGRESS	BUYS DRINKS FOR CO AND XO

LOGICAL	ARGUMENTATIVE
INDIFFERENT TO INSTRUCTION	KNOWS MORE THAN HIS SENIORS
STERN DISCIPLINARIAN	A BASTARD
TACTFUL IN DEALING WITH SUPERIORS	KNOWS WHEN TO KEEP HIS MOUTH SHUT
APPROACHES DIFFICULT PROBLEMS WITH EASE	FINDS SOMEONE ELSE TO DO THE JOB
A KEEN ANALYST	THOROUGHLY CONFUSED
DEFINITELY NOT THE DESK TYPE	DID NOT GO TO COLLEGE
EXPRESSES HIMSELF WELL	SPEAKS ENGLISH FLUENTLY
OFTEN SPENDS EXTRA HOURS ON THE JOB	MISERABLE HOME LIFE
A TRUE SOUTHERN GENTLEMAN	A HILLBILLY
CONSCIENTIOUS AND CAREFUL	SCARED
METICULOUS IN ATTENTION TO DETAIL	A NIT PICKER
DEMONSTRATES QUALITIES OF LEADERSHIP	HAS A LOUD VOICE
JUDGEMENT IS USUALLY SOUND	LUCKY
MAINTAINS PROFESSIONAL ATTITUDE	A SNOB
KEEN SENSE OF HUMOR	HAS A VAST REPERTOIRE OF DIRTY JOKES
STRONG ADHERENCE TO PRINCIPLES	STUBBORN
CAREER MINDED	HATES RESERVES
GETS ALONG WELL WITH SUPERIORS AND SUBOR- DINATES ALIKE	A COWARD
SLIGHTLY BELOW AVERAGE	STUPID
A VERY FINE OFFICER OF GREAT VALUE TO THE SERVICE	GETS TO WORK ON TIME

5. A Glossary of Nautical Terms

In contrast to the preceding definitions which sought to convey the hidden or true meanings of jargon, the present glossary is primarily concerned with making preposterous puns. While the title is quite similar to "A Glossary of Naval Terms" previously reported in WH, 51, the content is completely different. The following version was reported from a member of the crew of the Hughes Glomar Explorer at Long Beach, California, in 1975. A nearly identical version was collected from a Naval Reserve Officer in Washington, D.C., in 1976. For a Swedish variant, see MF, 53.

A GLOSSARY OF NAUTICAL TERMS

The two terms most commonly used in boating are "PORT and STARBOARD."

PORT—Facing the bow, "PORT" is on your left. It is easy to remember "PORT" has "four" letters, and "left" has "four" letters. So "PORT" is "Left."

STARBOARD—Since there are only two sides on a boat, and Port is one of them, it is obviously clear that the other one is left. So, "STARBOARD" is left.

Other Necessary Nautical Terms

AHEAD—The nautical term of "ajohn."

ASTERN—Without humor, i.e. "The Captain told no jokes. He was astern Captain."

AMIDSHIPS—This condition exists when you are completely surrounded by boats.

ANCHOR—What you display when you find you're completely surrounded by boats.

BERTH—The day on which you were born.

BUNK—Phony sea story.

BUOY—A buoy is the floating device you always smash into when trying to avoid the submerged obstacle the buoy is there to warn you about.

CHANNEL MARKER—Tells which station you're tuned into on your TV set.

DINGHY—The sounds of a ship's bells, i.e. "Dinghy-Dinghy-Dinghy-Dinghy."

DISPLACEMENT—Accidental loss, i.e. When you dock your boat and later you can't find it again, you've displaced it.

DOCK—Nickname for a medical man.

EDDY—Nelson's last name.

HEAVE-HO—What you do when you get seasick, and you've eaten too much ho.

HITCH—The thing to look for when a millionaire invites you on his boat . . . especially if you're a female.

KEEL—What your wife does to you when she finds you've bought a boat!

LAUNCH—The meal eaten aboard a boat about noontime.

MOOR—Amount of people needed for a boat-party, like, "The moor, the merrier."

OAR—When you have a choice, like "This . . . oar that!"

PORTHOLE—A hole in the left side of the boat—or is it the right side?

QUARTER-DECK—The floor on a cheap boat, which cost about 25¢ to install.

SHOAL—Worn by female sailors on chilly nights.

TIDE—A commercial detergent.

SUPERSTRUCTURE—A structure that's a lot better than the one on your boat.

WAKE—What your friends attend when you've been careless with your boat.

6. Useful Arabic Phrases

Travelers going abroad often seek easy language guidebooks which contain minimal vocabulary items or phrases. Normally, the phrases are polite formulas or standard questions relating to food, money, lodging, and the like. In the second half of the twentieth century, an increase in international terrorism has caused anxiety among travelers, particularly those headed for destinations in the Middle East. Hijackings and kidnappings have been featured prominently in the news media and hostages have been taken for long periods of time.

The following text, collected in Berkeley in 1988, reflects the fear of Americans traveling to the Middle East. The language supposedly being translated is not genuine Arabic. In fact, in another version collected in Berkeley in 1971, entitled "Trench Coat Humor" (and attributed to Peter Freundlich) we find the subtitle "Useful Farsi Phrases," thereby referring to Iran rather than the Arab world. The "Farsi" text includes two additional phrases which translate as "Kindly do me the honor of allowing me to kiss your behind" and "It is with the greatest pleasure that I sign this confession." There are other differences. For example, in the "Farsi" version, "Whatever you say!" is a translation from "Yu bhet" rather than "Balli, balli, balli!" Needless to say, "Yu bhet" (you bet) may be farcical, but it is definitely not Farsi.

USEFUL ARABIC PHRASES TO KNOW WHEN TRAVELLING ABROAD

Akbar khali-kili haftir lotfan.
Thank you for showing me your marvelous gun.

Fekr gabul cardan davat paeh gush divar.
I am delighted to accept your kind invitation to lie down on the floor with my arms above my head and my legs apart.

Shomaeh fekr tamomeh qeh gofteh bande.
I agree with everything you have ever said or thought of in your life.

Auto arraregh davateeman mano sepaheh-hast.
It is exceptionally kind of you to allow me to travel in the trunk of your car.

Fashal-eh tupehman na degat mano goftam cheesayeh mohema rajebehkeshvarehman.
If you will do me the kindness of not harming my genital appendages, I will gladly reciprocate by betraying my country in public.

Never Try to Teach a Pig to Sing

Khrel, jepaheh maneh va jayeii amrikaney.
I will tell you the names and addresses of many American
spies travelling as reporters.

Balli, balli, balli!
Whatever you say!

Maternier ghermez ahlieh, Ghorban.
The red blindfold would be lovely, Excellency.

*Tikeh nuneh ba ob khreleh bezorg va krube boyast ino
begeram.*
The water-soaked bread crumbs are delicious, thank you. I
must have the recipe.

*Etehfor'an dehratee, otageh shoma mikrastam khe do haftaeh
ba bodaneh Sheereel Teegz.*
Truly, I would rather be a hostage to your greatly esteemed self
than spend a fortnight in the arms of Cheryl Tiegs.

7. Official Polish (Italian) Sex Quiz

Stereotypes of peoples are just as common at home as abroad.
In the United States, there are well-known ethnic slur traditions
aimed at Polish-Americans or Italian-Americans. Invariably the
butt of these jokes is depicted as being ignorant. Some of these
stupid/dirty stereotypes are easily transferred to other groups in
other countries. For example, the English tell similar jokes about
the Irish, the French tell them about the Belgians, the Germans
tell them about East-Frisians, etc.

In the following text from Gaithersburg, Maryland, in the 1970s,
the stereotype takes the form of a purported test, and the ascribed
ignorance is primarily associated with sexual matters. For another
version, unfortunately a composite text, see *Maledicta* 9 (1986–87),
225–26. For a version not attributed to any particular ethnic group,
see Blanche Knott, *Truly Tasteless Jokes IV* (New York: Pinnacle
Books, 1984), p. 82. For a "Polish" version, see RJ, 106. For a version
entitled "Official Aggie 'Sex' Test," see Earl Fuller, *A Life Fuller
Laughter* (n.p., n.d.), pp. 67–69.

THE OFFICIAL POLISH SEX QUIZ

TRUE FALSE

1. A CLITORIS IS A TYPE OF FLOWER.

2. A PUBIC HAIR IS A WILD RABBIT.

3. A VULVA IS AN AUTOMOBILE FROM SWEDEN.

4. THE TERM "SPREAD EAGLE" IS AN EXTINCT BIRD.

5. A FALLOPIAN TUBE IS PART OF A TELEVISION.

6. IT IS DANGEROUS TO HAVE A WET DREAM UNDER AN ELECTRIC BLANKET.

7. COPULATION IS SEX BETWEEN TWO CONSENTING POLICEMEN.

8. McDONALD'S GOLDEN ARCHES IS A PHALLIC SYMBOL.

9. A VAGINA IS A MEDICAL TERM USED TO DESCRIBE HEART TROUBLE.

10. A MENSTRUAL CYCLE HAS THREE WHEELS.

11. FELLATIO IS AN ITALIAN DAGGER.

12. A G-STRING IS A WEAPON USED BY G-MEN.

13. SEMEN IS A TERM FOR SAILORS.

14. AN ANUS IS A GREEK WORD DENOTING A PERIOD OF TIME.

15. TESTICLES ARE FOUND ON AN OCTOPUS.

16. CUNNILINGUS IS A PERSON WHO CAN SPEAK 4 LANGUAGES.

17. ASPHALT IS A MEDICAL TERM USED TO DESCRIBE SOMEONE WITH RECTAL PROBLEMS.

18. KOTEX IS A RADIO STATION IN DALLAS, TEXAS.

19. MASTURBATE IS SOMETHING USED TO CATCH LARGE FISH.

20. COITUS IS A MUSICAL INSTRUMENT.

21. FETUS IS A CHARACTER ON GUNSMOKE.

22. AN UMBILICAL CORD IS PART OF A PARACHUTE.

23. A CONDOM IS AN APARTMENT COMPLEX.

24. A RECTUM IS WHAT YOU ARE TAKING THIS TEST.

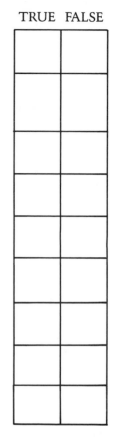

8. Definition of Diplomacy

Sometimes definitions are limited to a single word or concept. The following example was collected in Oakland, circa 1974. There are also oral definitions of the same term. For example, overheard at an IBM conference in Phoenix, Arizona, in May, 1989, was: "What's diplomacy? Diplomacy is to say 'Nice doggy, nice doggy,' until you find a stick."

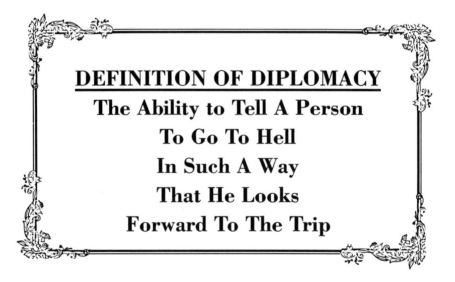

<u>DEFINITION OF DIPLOMACY</u>
The Ability to Tell A Person
To Go To Hell
In Such A Way
That He Looks
Forward To The Trip

9. Hell!

One four-letter word which has much less emotional impact than some others refers to that portion of the afterlife reserved for sinners. While not as explosive as four-letter words referring to sexual parts and processes, hell does qualify as a taboo word. The existence of such euphemisms as "heck" attest to its taboo status, at least in former times. The incredible utility of this catch-all epithet is well illustrated in the following folk poem collected in San Francisco in 1971 but reported to have circulated in 1938–39 in Cedar Rapids, Iowa. In *Immortalia*, a privately published collection of bawdy folk and literary verse, the authorship of "Hell" is attributed to E. A. von Kleim. See *Immortalia* ([New York], 1927), p. 127. Legman suggests that *Immortalia* was probably edited by T. R. Smith, editor of *Poetica Erotica*. See. G. Legman, *The Horn Book* (New Hyde Park: University Books, 1964), p. 394.

HELL!

Just what is meant by this word "Hell?"
They say sometimes "it's cold as hell."
Sometimes they say "it's hot as hell."
When it rains hard "It's Hell" they cry.
It's also "Hell" when it is dry
They "Hate like Hell" to see it snow
It's "A Hell of a wind" when it starts to blow,
Now "How in Hell" can anyone tell
"What in Hell" they mean by this word "Hell"
This married life is "Hell" they say.
When he comes in late, it's "hell to pay"
When he starts to yell it's a "Hell of a note".
It's "Hell" when the kid you've got to tote
It's "Hell" when the doctor sends his bills
For a "Hell of a lot" of trips and pills
When you get this you'll know real well
Just what is meant by this word "Hell".
"Hell yes!", "Hell no!", and "Oh Hell" too,
"The Hell you don't", "The Hell you do"
And "What in Hell!" and "The Hell of it is"
"The Hell with yours," and "The Hell with his!"
Now "Who in Hell!" and "Oh, Hell, where"
And "What the Hell do you think I care?"
But "the Hell of it is" "It's sure as Hell"
We don't know "What in Hell" is "Hell".

10. Patience

The following definition was collected in Dublin, California, in 1980. It has to do with the need for patience and self-control in a world which is full of stress and provocation. American culture with its emphasis upon speed makes it perhaps more difficult for Americans to restrain themselves than members of other cultures accustomed to waiting patiently in a queue.

Patience is the ability to idle your motor when you feel like stripping your gears.

11. God, Grant Me Patience

The contrast between patience and impatience is dramatically illustrated in the following text from San Rafael, California, in 1978.

GOD, GRANT ME PATIENCE . . .
AND I WANT IT RIGHT NOW !

12. The New Priest

Vocabularies differ with respect to formal and informal social settings. It is usually a mistake to use informal language in a formal situation. In this instance, the linguistic breaches of etiquette are presumably the results of alcoholic influence. The version presented here was collected in Berkeley in 1974. Legman cites a 1968 version from Los Angeles (NLM, 763) and also indicates one of the lines (the allusion to St. Taffy's Church) is a separate item dating from 1938 (RDJ, 158). This line, according to Carol Mitchell, is interpreted differently by men and by women. Men understand the line as a pleasurable experience while many women assumed an implication of castration. See Carol Mitchell, "The Sexual Perspective in the Appreciation and Interpretation of Jokes," *Western Folklore* 36 (1977), 326–28.

For other versions, see *Playboy's Party Jokes 6* (New York: PBJ Books, 1974), and Blanche Knott, *Truly Tasteless Jokes 3* (New York: Ballantine Books, 1983), pp. 96–97. For an English version, see RIF, 122.

THE NEW PRIEST

A new priest at his first Mass was so scared he couldn't even speak. After Mass, he asked the Monsignor how he had done. The Monsignor said, "Fine, but next week it might help if you put vodka or a little gin in your water glass to help relax you."

The next Sunday the priest put vodka in his glass and really talked up a storm. After Mass he again asked the Monsignor how he had done. The Monsignor said, "Fine, but that there were a few things they should get straightened out."

1. There are 10 Commandments . . . not 12.
2. There are 12 Disciples . . . not 10.
3. David slew Goliath. He didn't kick the shit out of him.
4. We do not refer to Jesus Christ as the "late J.C."
5. And next Sunday there is a taffy pulling contest at St. Peters, NOT a peter pulling contest at St. Taffys.
6. The Father, Son and The Holy Ghost are not referred to as: Big Daddy, Junior and Spook.

The play on "taffy pulling contest at St. Peters" is reminiscent of a standard oral joke in which Catholic priests become tongue-tied when confronted with a buxom young woman dressed inappropriately. In one version, three priests in Grand Central Station in New York City try in succession to buy tickets from such a woman. The first asks for "three pickets for Titsburgh." The second does request three tickets for Pittsburgh, but then falters as he continues, "And I'd like my change in nipples and dimes." The third priest, the oldest, succeeds in asking for the tickets and change, but then he tries to admonish her for her provocative dress. He concludes by warning her that when she one day passes to the Great Beyond, "St. Finger will certainly be there pointing his peter at you." See Andrew L. Cleveland, *Dirty Stories for All Occasions* (New York: Galahad Books, 1980), pp. 78–79. For a shorter version, see Julius Alvin, *Extremely Gross Jokes*, Vol. IV (New York: Zebra Books, 1985), p. 87.

Never Try to Teach a Pig to Sing

13. The Play

Another type of urban folklore which deals with the playful use of language concerns the inability of an actor to articulate a word or phrase. In this sense, the items are analogous to tongue-twisters or spooneristic conundrums. (For examples of spooneristic conundrums, see Alan Dundes and Robert A. Georges, "Some Minor Genres of Obscene Folklore," *Journal of American Folklore* 75 [1962], 222.) In theory, these linguistic routines could be entirely in oral tradition, but in practice they are often encountered in the office copier format. Since these materials commonly depend for their impact upon the taboos against uttering obscenities in public, they illustrate the continuing apprehension of American children and adults with respect to exposure to "dirty words."

For other versions, see NLM, 809, UFFC-TB, 150–51, and RIF, 116. For an interesting variant in which the nervous actor practices his one line offstage, "Hark, hear the cannon roar!," but once on stage upon hearing the loud blast of the cannon exclaims "What the fuck was that?" see Sidney Spite and Johnny Lyons, *Joking Off V* (Toronto: PaperJacks, 1988), pp. 15–16.

The Play

Two small boys of grammer school age, were in thier 1st school play. Each had a small part. The 1st boy was to say, "Oh my Fair Maiden, I have come to snatch a kiss and fill your soul with hope"!

The 2nd was to say "Hark a pistol shot"!

The night of the play the boy's parents were on the front row seats and they were very nervous. As the curtain rose the 1st stepped forward in a loud voice and said, "Oh my Fair maiden, I have come to kiss your snatch and fill your hole with soap." This made the 2nd one more nervous and he said, "Hark the shistel pot, pistol shit, shit pot, cow shit, Oh bull shit, I didn't want to be in this god damn play anyway."

The End

14. The Pissed-Off Cowboy

The contrast between genteel and vulgar language is a popular subject in urban folklore. While the genteel typically object to hearing foul language spoken in their presence, the folk generally tend to reverse this—strenuously objecting to euphemistic circumlocutions. Sometimes the genteel/vulgar dichotomy involves sexual stereotyping. The woman is, of course, depicted as pristine and polite, the man as coarse and vulgar. The following text was collected in Costa Mesa, California, in 1976. Legman reports an oral text collected in Brooklyn in 1949. See RDJ, 235. For other texts, see NLM, 711, and Blanche Knott, *Truly Tasteless Jokes IV* (New York: Pinnacle Books, 1984), p. 78.

THE PISSED OFF COWBOY

Shortly after the roundup, the cattle were rounded into the cattle cars and shipped to Chicago for sale. Each car had an attendant to feed and water the cattle on the journey. This is the story of one such cowboy.

Following the unloading of the cattle in Chicago, the cowboy headed for a restaurant for dinner. The only seat left was next to a young lady about 20 years old who looked wealthy and well educated. He couldn't help overhearing her place her order—"I'll have breast of fowl—virgin fowl—make sure it's virgin—catch it yourself; garnish my plate with onions and bring me a coffee, not too hot, and not too cold; and Waiter—open the window, I smell a horse, there must be a cowboy in the house."

Thoroughly pissed off, the cowboy placed his order like this:
"I'll have Duck—fucked Duck—make sure it's fucked—fuck it yourself; garnish my plate with horse shit. Then bring me a cup of coffee as strong as Texas Mule Piss, and blow the foam off with a fart, and Waiter—knock down the wall—I smell a Cunt, there must be a Whore in the house."

15. What Not to Name Your Dog

This item which is found coast to coast plays at some length on an extended double entendre. This particular text is from Oakland in 1987. In another version from Michigan circa 1981 (not presented here), there is an additional introductory paragraph as follows:

> For protection, my father bought me a German Shepherd Dog. When he found out I was Jewish, he bit me. He was a wonderful watchdog. One evening while I was being held up, he watched.

"WHAT NOT TO NAME YOUR DOG"

Everybody who has a dog calls him "Rover" or "Boy."
I call mine "Sex."
Now, Sex has been very embarrassing to me.
When I went to City Hall to renew his dog license, I told the clerk that I would like a license for Sex.

He said, "I'd like to have one, too."
Then I said, "You don't understand. I've had Sex since I was nine years old."
He said, "You must have been quite a kid!"

When I got married and went on my honeymoon, I took the dog with me.

I told the hotel clerk that I wanted a room for my wife and me, and a special room for Sex. He said, "Every room in the place is for sex." I said, "You don't understand. Sex keeps me awake at night." The clerk said, "Me, too."

One day I entered Sex in a contest, but before the competition began, the dog ran away. Another contestant asked me why I was just standing there looking around. I told him I had planned to have Sex in the contest. He told me that I should have sold tickets. "But you don't understand," I said. "I had hoped to have Sex on T.V." He called me a show-off.

When my wife and I separated, we went to court to fight for custody of the dog. I said, "Your Honor, I had Sex before I was married." The judge said, "Me, too." Then I told him that after I was married, Sex left me. He said, "Me, too."

Never Try to Teach a Pig to Sing

Last night Sex ran off again. I spent hours looking around town for him. A cop came over to me and asked, "What are you doing in the alley at 4 o'clock in the morning?" I said, "I'm looking for Sex."

My case comes up Friday.

16. Lost Dog

Man's best friend is supposedly his dog, but humans do not always treat their pets kindly. The rise of the animal rights movement in the United States with its vocal opposition to cruelty to laboratory animals used in scientific research has focused public attention on the issue.

The question of whether or not pets should be neutered is a debatable one, just as birth control in general is. One could argue that it is responsible pet owners who neuter their cats and dogs as opposed to pet owners who let their animals run free thereby producing strays and unwanted litters.

If one thinks that pets sometimes take the place of children in family life, then the mistreatment of pets may correspond to child abuse. In the following two texts, both from Marin County, California, in the late 1980s, there is at least the possibility that a mistreated dog may have left home intentionally. In any case, the contrast between the dog's condition and his name provides the humor. It also suggests the American penchant for Polyanna's rose-colored optimism, even in the face of obvious misfortune. The interesting variation in these two texts demonstrates the nature of multiple existence in photocopier folklore.

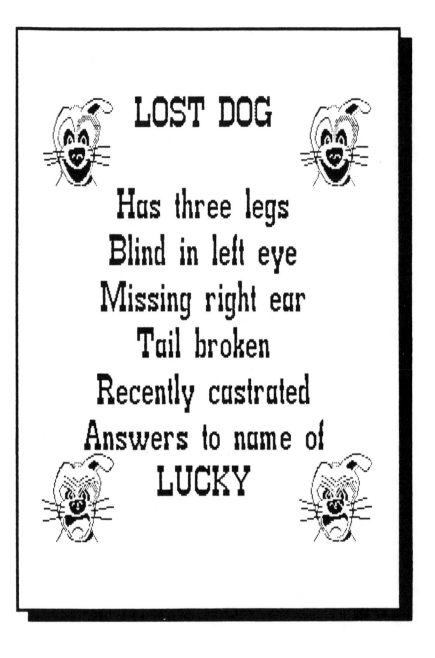

Never Try to Teach a Pig to Sing

LOST DOG

Description:

3 LEGS
BLIND IN LEFT EYE
MISSING RIGHT EAR
TAIL BROKEN
ACCIDENTALLY
NEUTERED...
ANSWERS TO NAME OF
"LUCKY"

17. Stress

If there is one feature omnipresent in urban life, it is surely stress. There is stress in family life, in commuting, in one's work. Stress has even been recognized as a serious matter by the medical world. Ways of reducing stress are taught in workshops. They include various forms of exercise and meditation. In the following text collected from Nestlé Foods Corporation in Ripon, California, we find a blunt, earthy definition of stress. Most versions of this item do not include the accompanying cartoon, recognizable as Berkeley Breathed's Bill the Cat.

The second unrelated item also uses an animal to illustrate the effects of stress. The idea of becoming unglued or perhaps unstrung is suggested by the zebra's plight. The surrealistic image of the zebra's hind legs being tied together by the loose stripes heightens the crippling nature of severe stress. The caption seems slightly odd inasmuch as a more idiomatic expression might refer to "undergoing" stress or "suffering" from a stress attack. The item was collected in Stockton, California, in October, 1989.

"STRESS"

THE CONFUSION CREATED WHEN ONE'S MIND OVERRIDES THE BODY'S BASIC DESIRE TO CHOKE THE LIVING SHIT OUT OF SOME ASSHOLE WHO DESPERATELY NEEDS IT!

I THINK I'M HAVING STRESS!

Never Try to Teach a Pig to Sing

18. Twenty-six Ways to Relieve Stress

Once stress was officially recognized by the medical establishment as being a factor contributing to the onset of heart attacks, ulcers, and other diseases, it was only a question of time before the folk would suggest techniques to alleviate it. The following item was collected in Fishersville, Virginia, in 1989.

26 WAYS TO RELIEVE STRESS

1. Pop some popcorn without putting the lid on the popper.
2. Drive to work in reverse.
3. Pay your electric bill in pennies.
4. Write a memo to your boss in Pig Latin.
5. When someone says, "have a nice day," tell them you've made other plans.
6. Learn to weasel buff.
7. Put your kid's goldfish in a blender and hit the "on" switch.
8. Put a toad in a microwave oven.
9. Send a candy gram to your favorite diet center.
10. Make a "Things To Do List" of all the things you've already done.
11. Dance naked in front of your house pets.
12. Put your toddler's clothes on backwards and send him to preschool as if nothing is wrong.
13. Fill out your tax forms in Roman Numerals.
14. Page through the National Geographic magazine and draw underwear on the natives.
15. Go shopping. Buy everything. Sweat in them and return them the next day.
16. Tell your boss to blow it out his mule, then let him figure it out.
17. Read a dictionary upside down and look for secret messages.
18. Start a nasty rumor and see if you recognize it when it gets back to you.
19. Write a short story using alphabet soup.
20. Paste a picture of your boss on the center-fold of a Playgirl magazine and send it to his wife.

21. Stare at people through a fork and pretend they're in jail.
22. Make-up a language and ask people for directions.
23. Dress up as Rambo for your daughter's wedding.
24. Super Glue your boss's coffee cup to his desk and fill it up.
25. Send an application for night school to your instructor.
26. Put a waitress's tip in a glass of water, then turn it upside down on the table.

19. Stress Diet

One possible way of relieving stress is through diet. Dieting in the United States has become more than a fad; it has become a national way of life for many individuals. A cursory look at the diet book section of any major bookstore will show the range of different diet plans available.

Few Americans are able to stick to a diet. Most individuals go on and off diets at various times in their lives. Some lose weight, but then discover to their dismay that they have gained all or some of it back. The following text from the Stoneridge American Telephone and Telegraph office in Pleasanton, California, in 1987, demonstrates the discrepancy between starting and staying on a diet. It should be noted that the very act of dieting probably produces a fair amount of stress in most individuals. One response to stress is eating, even compulsive eating.

STRESS DIET

BREAKFAST

½ grapefruit
1 slice whole wheat toast
8 oz. skim milk

LUNCH

4 oz. lean broiled chicken breast
1 cup steamed zucchini
1 Oreo cookie
Herb Tea

MID-AFTERNOON SNACK

Rest of the package of Oreos
1 quart Rocky Road Ice Cream
1 Jar Hot Fudge

DINNER

2 loaves garlic bread
Large pepperoni and mushroom pizza
Large pitcher of beer
3 Milky Way candy bars
Entire frozen cheesecake directly from freezer

DIET TIPS

1. If no one sees you eat it, it has no calories.
2. If you drink a diet soda with a candy bar they cancel each other out.
3. When eating with someone, calories don't count if you both eat the same amount.
4. Food used for medicinal purposes NEVER counts, such as: Hot Chocolate, Brandy, Toast, and Sara Lee Cheesecake.
5. If you fatten up everyone else around you—then you look thinner.
6. Movie related foods don't count because they are simply part of the entire entertainment experience and not a part of one's personal fuel such as Milk Duds, Popcorn with butter, Junior Mints, and Red Licorice.

In a second version from Berkeley in 1987 (not presented here) entitled "Dieting Under Stress," there are three additional "Rules for this Diet" (i.e., Diet Tips):

7. Cookie pieces contain no calories. The process of breaking causes calorie leakage.
8. Things licked off of knives and spoons have no calories if you are in the process of preparing something. Examples are peanut butter on a knife making a sandwich and ice cream on a spoon making a sunday.
9. Foods that have the same color have the same number of calories. Examples are spinach and pistachio ice cream, mushrooms and white chocolate. NOTE: chocolate is a universal color and may be substituted for any other food color.

For a version published in England, see RJ, 86–87.

20. Recipe for Stuffed Camel

The American craze for dieting is paralleled by an equally strong penchant for eating, even over-eating, that is, stuffing oneself. The large number of diet books in American bookstores is exceeded only by the large number of cookbooks. These cookbooks from a worldwide variety of cultures feature exotic cuisines of all description. Foods which were largely unknown to most Americans a few short years ago are now accepted parts of American culinary fare, especially in cities. The influx of new immigrants to American shores has also expanded the range of dining possibilities. However, some foods continue to remain alien to American taste. The first version of the following recipe collected in the Bay Area in 1987 presents an unlikely dish for a very sizeable dinner party. Structurally speaking, it is interesting that the recipe is analogous to a formula folktale (or to the famous Russian wooden doll sets in which one doll fits into the next larger size doll). The second version was collected in Berkeley, circa 1959.

RECIPE FOR STUFFED CAMEL

1 medium camel
4 lambs
20 chickens (roasted)
150 eggs (boiled)
40 kilos tomatoes
Salt and seasonings

Stuff eggs into tomatoes
Stuff tomatoes into chickens
Stuff chickens into lambs
Stuff lambs into camel

Roast until tender

Serves 150 people

Roast Camel

| 1 camel | 1 sheep carcass | 3 chickens |
| 6 fish | 18 eggs | 1 wedding |

Hard boil eggs. Stuff eggs into fish. Fry fish. Broil chickens. Stuff fish into chickens. Roast sheep carcass. Stuff chickens into sheep carcass. Roast camel. Stuff sheep into camel. Serve at wedding. Serves 100.

21. Elephant Stew

Americans love exaggeration in their humor. The tall tale continues to be a favorite genre—the bigger the better. In the following recipe parody collected in Gaithersburg, Maryland, in the 1970s, the final punning punch line is reminiscent of shaggy dog stories. For a discussion of the latter genre, see Jan Harold Brunvand, "A Classification for Shaggy Dog Stories," *Journal of American Folklore* 76 (1963), 42–68. For the tall tale, see Carolyn S. Brown, *The Tall Tale in American Folklore and Literature* (Knoxville: University of Tennessee Press, 1987).

ELEPHANT STEW

2 Rabbits (Optional)
1 Elephant, Medium Size
Salt & Pepper to taste
Brown Gravy

Cut elephant into small bite-sized pieces. This should take about two months. Add enough brown gravy to cover. Cook over kerosene fire for about four weeks at 465°. This will serve 3800 people. If more are expected, two rabbits may be added, but do this only if necessary as some people do not like to find a hare in their stew.

22. Best Ever Rum Cake

Food and drink go together. Excessive drinking is perhaps even more of a problem in American society than excessive eating. Excessive eaters, after all, are rarely a threat to anyone but themselves. This is unfortunately not the case with excessive drinkers, especially those who drive automobiles "under the influence."

In the following recipe for rum cake, food and drink are combined. Dessert, normally one of the concluding highlights of any fine meal, may require considerable expertise in its preparation. The theme of progressive intoxication is common enough in office copier folklore (cf. "I Had Twelve Bottles" in WY, 69–71). This text collected from a Pacific Bell office in Bishop Ranch Industrial Park in San Ramon, California, in 1988 ends with two closing sentences referring to a business context. (Not all versions have this ending.)

Never Try to Teach a Pig to Sing

BEST EVER RUM CAKE

1 Tsp. Sugar	1 or 2 Quarts of Rum
1 Cup Dried Fruit	Brown Sugar
1 Tsp. Soda	1 Cup Butter
2 Large Eggs	Baking Powder
Lemon Juice	Nuts

Before starting, sample rum to check quality. Good, isn't it? Now proceed. Select large mixing bowl, measuring cup, etc. Check rum again. It must be just right. To be sure rum is of proper quality, pour one level cup of rum into a glass and drink it as fast as you can. Repeat. With electric mixer, beat 1 cup of butter in a large fluffy bowl. Add 1 seaspoon of thugar and beat again. Meanwhile, make sure rum is still alright. Try another cup. Open second quart if necessary. Add leggs, 2 cups of fried druit and beat till high. if druit gets stuck in beaters, pry loose with drewscriber. Sample rum again, checking for tonscisticity. Next, sift 3 cups pepper or salt (really doesn't matter). Sample rum. Sift ½ pint lemon juice. Fold in chopped butter and strained nuts. Add 1 bablespoon of brown sugar—or whatever color you can find. Wix mell. Grease oven. Turn cake pan to 350 gredees. Pour mess into boven and ake. Check rum again and bo to ged.

Bank you for your thisness. See you at the vocention in Befruary.

23. Fishin' Line

An imaginary dialogue between two fisherman is the subject of a distinctive folkloristic tradition. The economy and slurring of words suggests the individualism and isolation of each fisherman. Greetings and minimal critical information are exchanged after which each is free to go his own separate way. This version was collected on Vashon Island in Washington state in 1970. In another version, the title is "When Fisherman Meet."

The extent to which some men are devoted to recreational fishing is the subject of a second item collected from a Union Pacific Railroad employee in California in April 1990. In this tongue-in-cheek want ad notice, fishing takes precedence over everything.

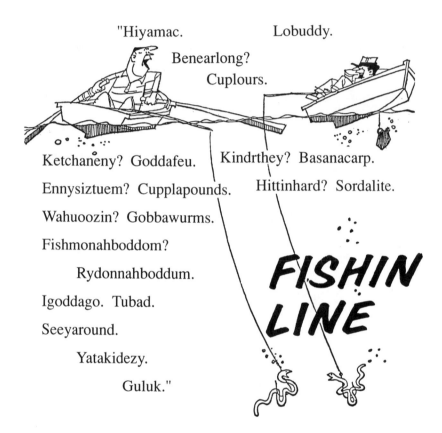

"Hiyamac.   Lobuddy.

Benearlong?
Cuplours.

Ketchaneny? Goddafeu.   Kindrthey? Basanacarp.

Ennysiztuem? Cupplapounds.   Hittinhard? Sordalite.

Wahuoozin? Gobbawurms.

Fishmonahboddom?

Rydonnahboddum.

Igoddago. Tubad.

Seeyaround.

Yatakidezy.

Guluk."

FISHIN LINE

WANTED

GOOD WOMAN

must be able to
CLEAN - COOK - SEW
Dig Worms
and
Clean Fish

MUST HAVE BOAT and MOTOR

please send picture
of
boat and motor

24. In Honour Of National Condom Week

With the advent of public discussions of birth control, it was inevitable that specifics would be mentioned. Normally a taboo subject, condoms have been widely mentioned in the media as part of the national response to the dangers of Acquired Immune Deficiency Syndrome (AIDS). In the United States, thanks to intensive legislative lobbying in Washington, D.C., there are days, weeks, and months designated to honor products, events, and groups. Sometimes, these legislated time periods are marked by an official slogan.

In the following text collected on the campus of the University of California, Davis, in 1988, we have a parody of such honorific events in the form of a list of proposed slogans. The spelling of "honor" with a "u" indicates that this particular version may have originated in England. The small cartoon drawing with its smiling face suggests that the subject of condom use in connection with the prevention of AIDS and other sexually transmitted diseases is no longer so taboo. This is also indicated by public displays in drugstores and public pronouncements by the Surgeon-General of the United States and other senior public health officials.

While condoms may no longer be such a taboo topic, sexually transmitted diseases are another matter. There is still a stigma attached, in the public mind, to individuals who find themselves infected with such a disease. This is the subject of the second text, which was collected in St. Charles, Missouri, in April 1990. For purposes of practical joking, the item would bear the name and address of a particular "victim."

IN HONOUR OF NATIONAL CONDOM WEEK
OUR LITTLE FRIEND "ROBBIE RUBBER"
REMINDS US TO:

1. Cover your stump before you hump
2. Before you attack her, cover your whacker
3. Don't be silly, protect your willie
4. Before you blast her, guard your bushmaster
5. Don't be a loner, cover your boner
6. When in doubt, shroud your spout
7. You can't go wrong, if you shield your dong
8. If you ain't gonna sack it, go home and whack it
9. If you think she's spunkey, cover your monkey
10. Before you bag her, sheath your dagger
11. It'll be sweeter, if you wrap your peter
12. If you slip between thighs, be sure to condomize
13. Save embarrassment later, cover your gator
14. She won't get sick, if you cap your dick
15. If you go into heat, package your meat
16. While you're undressing Venus, dress up your penis
17. Off with her pants and blouse? Suit up the trouser mouse
18. Never deck her with an unwrapped pecker
19. Especially in December, gift wrap your member
20. She'll do cunnilingus with a shielded dingus, and be into fellatio if you wrap your Horatio
21. Befo' the van start rockin', be sho' yo' cock gets a stockin'
22. Don't be a fool, Vulcanize your tool
23. The right selection? Sack that erection
24. Wrap it in foil before checking her oil
25. A crank with armour will never harm her

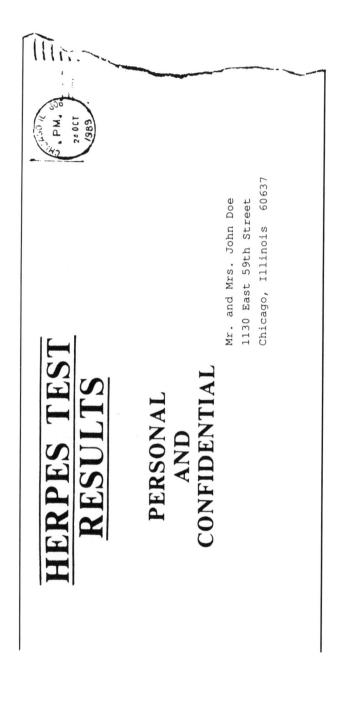

HERPES TEST RESULTS

PERSONAL AND CONFIDENTIAL

Mr. and Mrs. John Doe
1130 East 59th Street
Chicago, Illinois 60637

25. This . . . Really Bothers You

The epidemic proportions of AIDS has had a drastic impact upon sexual activity among both homosexual and heterosexual individuals. The fear of contracting AIDS, an incurable and fatal disease, has definitely inhibited sexual activity of all kinds. The large number of jokes about AIDS demonstrates the extent to which consciousness of this dread disease has been raised among the folk.

A typical joke goes as follows: Mr. Johnson concerned about his wife who has undergone a series of tests at a local hospital calls her doctor to get the results of the tests. The doctor informs him that there were two Mrs. Johnsons who were tested at the hospital on the same day, and their records unfortunately got mixed up. One of the Mrs. Johnsons has Alzheimer's disease and the other has AIDS. The husband asks, "What shall I do?" The doctor inquires, "Is your wife home now?" The husband says, "Yes." The doctor advises, "Take her a couple of blocks from home and leave her. If she finds her way home, don't screw her!"

Another popular joke describes a young man who goes to a doctor for a physical examination. The doctor tells him that he has AIDS. After an emotional outburst, the youth asks the doctor, "Is there anything I can do?" The doctor consoles him by saying that he will get the best medical care available, round-the-clock nursing service, and to start immediately a diet of flounder and pancakes. The boy asks, "Oh, is that a cure for AIDS?" "No, but they are the only things we can slide under the door." In another version of this joke, the diet consists of salsa and hot chili peppers (and/or the doctor urges the boy to travel to Mexico where he is to drink the water and eat unwashed fresh vegetables). The boy asks the same question and the doctor responds, "No, but it will teach you what your asshole is really for." For a variant of this second joke, see Blanche Knott, *Truly Tasteless Jokes VII* (New York: St. Martin's Press, 1987), p. 40. For other AIDS jokes, see Casper G. Schmidt, "AIDS Jokes, or, *Schadenfreude* around an Epidemic," *Maledicta* 8 (1984–85), 69–75; Alan Dundes, "At Ease, Disease—AIDS Jokes as Sick Humor," *American Behavorial Scientist* 30 (1987), 72–81; and Joseph P. Goodwin, Unprintable Reactions to All the News That's Fit to Print," *Southern Folklore* 46 (1989), 15–39.

The following text was collected in Walnut Creek, California, in 1989, and it demonstrates the fear of AIDS among newlyweds as well as the results of a national campaign promoting the use of condoms for safe sex. For a variant of this cartoon, see Reinhold Aman, "Kakologia: A Chronicle of Nasty Riddles and Naughty Wordplays," *Maledicta* 9 (1986–87), 297.

THIS AIDS SHIT REALLY BOTHERS YOU.

Never Try to Teach a Pig to Sing

26. T-Shirt Quotes

Although there are many T-shirts which have slogans or aphorisms stamped or imprinted on them, it is by no means certain that all of the following thirty-one quotations have actually appeared on T-shirts. They are a mixture of proverbs and one-liners from a variety of sources and possessing differing degrees of traditionality. "Beam me up, Scotty . . ." derives from the popular television show "Star Trek." Some are parodies, e.g., of the proverb "Time flies" or of the homily "It's not whether you win or lose, it's how you play the game." We note that the list of quotes includes the expression which we selected for the title of this volume. The text was collected in Oakland in 1983.

T-SHIRT QUOTES

1. "Beam me up, Scotty, there's no intelligent life down here."
2. "Pardon me, but you've obviously mistaken me for someone who gives a shit."
3. "Time flies when you don't know what you're doing."
4. "If you love something set it free, and if it doesn't come back to you, hunt it down and kill it."
5. "We are the people our parents warned us about."
6. "I'm not playing hard to get, I am hard to get."
7. "Those of you who think you know everything are very annoying to us who do."
8. "Never try to teach a pig to sing—it wastes your time and annoys the pig."
9. "I'd like to help you out. Which way did you come in?"
10. "How can I love you if you won't lie down?"
11. "How can I miss you if you won't go away?"
12. "Everyone needs to believe in something—I believe I will have another beer."
13. "I'd rather be pissed off than pissed on."
14. "I'm not deaf, I'm ignoring you."
15. "How can I tell you I love you when you're sitting on my face?"
16. "It's not whether you win or lose, it's how you look playing the game."
17. "N-O . . . read my lips."
18. "Life is a bitch. Then you die."

19. "I don't have a drinking problem—I drink, I get drunk, I fall down. No problem."
20. "When I'm good I'm very good, but when I'm bad I'm better."
21. "Everyone wants to go to heaven, but no one wants to die."
22. "Whatever you do will be insignificant, but it's very important that you do it."
23. "Sex is the most fun you can have without laughing."
24. "Perfect paranoia is perfect awareness."
25. "I wish you were a beer."
26. "The one who dies with the most toys wins."
27. "I really appreciate your sincere criticism—fuck you very much."
28. "Experience is what you get when you didn't get what you wanted."
29. "Sex is like snow . . . you never know many inches or how long it'll last."
30. "If God had wanted us to go nude, we would have been born that way."
31. "Never attribute to malice what can be adequately explained by stupidity."

Signs of the Times

One of the easiest ways of collecting photocopier folklore is to walk unannounced into any office and inspect the walls or the desks or the bulletin boards in that office. Chances are that sooner or later one will encounter signs of the times. These signs run the gamut from inspirational to wry critiques of daily office routine. Since most of these signs are publicly displayed, they are on the whole somewhat less offensive than the items which circulate person to person in an office. Also as they tend to be fairly short, we have included a broader selection of examples than other types of copier folklore. Many items consist of no more than a sentence or two.

Because of their relative simplicity and non-offensive nature, these signs of the times are frequently chosen as the subjects of commercial wall plaques and certificates. However, the number of photocopied specimens of these signs far outnumber the commercial plaques. Plaques cost money whereas the photocopier versions are either free or minimally expensive.

The subjects treated by the signs are almost invariably complaints about office life. The themes include incompetent, inefficient fellow personnel, the necessity of keeping up appearances, poor planning, time pressures, unwelcome advice and criticism, answering dumb questions, and worries about being fired. These legitimate employee concerns cannot always be articulated directly. The signs offer a convenient impersonal safety valve for venting anger and frustration.

27. Never Try to Teach a Pig to Sing

Sometimes employees feel (rightfully) that they have been given a hopeless and futile task to accomplish. Management is not always correct. Still the faithful worker may feel obliged to plug away even if in his opinion it amounts to hitting his head against a stone wall. A good worker takes pride in being efficient and resents having to waste precious time on an unproductive assignment or what is deemed simply busywork.

The striking metaphor of trying to teach a pig to sing sums up the employee's view of a fool's errand. Although the sign may occur without a drawing (see item 26, "T-Shirt Quotes," above), we have elected to reproduce the following text collected in Torrance, California, in 1988. Another version, including a similar cartoon, was collected in Palo Alto in 1983. (The text below bears the name Greenwald.) For another version with a different cartoon image of the pig, see YD [33]. For English versions, see OHB, 21 and RJ, 42.

As to the vexing question why an employer would knowingly assign a useless task which has little or no chance of being successfully carried out, we may call upon another item of xerographic folklore, an item collected from the Kaiser Cement plant at Permanente, California, in June, 1989:

WEILER'S LAW:

Nothing is impossible for the man who doesn't have to do it himself.

Never try to teach a pig to sing,
it wastes your time and it annoys the pig.

28. It's Difficult to Soar with Eagles

The personnel of an office sometimes think of themselves as a unit or team. Such teams are no stronger than their weakest members. Diligent employees may resent less able co-workers whose inadequate efforts tend to bring down the level of achievement of the entire office. They may even consider that such incompetent colleagues ultimately cause them to do more work than necessary in order to correct the errors made by these less-skilled employees.

One common slang term for an incompetent is "turkey." A turkey, at least the domestic variety, is thought to be a particularly dumb bird. Whether this is true or not, the slang term with its pejorative connotations surely does exist. We present here three texts to show that variation can occur with respect to the text as well as the cartoon. The first two texts were collected in the Bay Area in 1980–81. The third from Fishersville, Virginia, in 1989, is noteworthy for having incorporated computerized graphics. For other versions, see OHB, 20; YD [80]; RJ, 20.

IT'S DIFFICULT TO
SOAR WITH EAGLES
WHEN YOU
WORK WITH
TURKEYS!

IT'S DIFFICULT
to Soar with Eagles
when you
Work with Turkeys!

It's hard to soar with
EAGLES,
When you work with
a bunch of
TURKEYS

29. The Rat Race Is Over

If turkeys are deemed stupid, rats are considered to be smart. They survive, often under difficult conditions. The phrase "rat race" connotes a combination of drudgery and competition. It is a decidedly negative image of the workplace suggesting that it is something to be endured, not enjoyed. According to Harold Wentworth and Stuart Berg Flexner's *Dictionary of American Slang* (New York: Thomas Y. Crowell, 1967). one possible source for the metaphor is the practice of laboratory rodents being placed on a treadmill to measure their energy. A race on a treadmill is a fruitless one since no matter how much energy is expended, one makes no progress. By analogy, a worker who toils at a machine or desk day after day does so without visible or tangible results. The following example which literalizes the metaphor comes from Sacramento in 1979. For other versions (with different drawings of the rat), see YD [94] and RJ, 30.

THE RAT RACE
IS OVER...

the rats won

Never Try to Teach a Pig to Sing

30. Don't Drink Water

Environmentalists have drawn attention to the hazards surrounding nearly everyone. The air we breathe, the food we eat, the water we drink are all suspect. Each day brings a new alarming report of some toxic or carcinogenic substance threatening the health of humankind. While some of these dangers are real enough, it is also true that exaggerated claims have been made, claims which do little more than trivialize the genuine problems. It becomes increasingly difficult for the general public to know which substances are perfectly safe to ingest, which drugs have no addictive or deleterious side effects whatsoever, and so on. The following sign is a commentary by the folk on the *reductio ad absurdum* of overstating environmental hazards. It was collected at an Air Force base near Sacramento in 1978.

Don't Drink Water
FISH FUCK IN IT!!

31. Be Like a Duck

Appearances are important in offices as in life. Generally speaking, it is considered desirable to seem serene and dignified even when one is in the midst of crisis. The dichotomy between appearance and reality is nicely illustrated in the following two texts. Above the waterline is appearance; below the waterline is reality. The texts demonstrate significant variation with respect to both the captions and the duck figures. The first text was collected in Palo Alto in 1976 while the second came from Carlisle, Pennsylvania, in 1980. For two additional versions, see UFFC-PC, 95–96; for an English version, see TCB, 58.

Be like a duck ....

ABOVE THE SURFACE LOOK CALM AND UNRUFFLED.......
BELOW THE SURFACE PADDLE LIKE HELL

Never Try to Teach a Pig to Sing

The secret of success is to stay cool and calm on top and paddle like HELL underneath!

32. A Moving Experience

The discrepancy between appearance and reality can also be signaled by flowery language masking an earthy activity. In this text collected from Gaithersburg, Maryland, in the 1970s, we find the popular fetish for natural laxatives combined with an advertising mailing technique in which recipients are informed they have won a valuable prize. Supposedly, the effects of prune juice and bran flakes are being compared using human subjects. The punning language is appropriately euphemistic. Americans definitely prefer not to be explicit about defecation. Typical advertising makes reference to "regularity" and the "gentleness" of laxatives. The print style of the text confirms the gentility of the invitation.

Congratulations!

You have been selected by Consumer Labs, Inc.

to participate in a special panel test

to determine the relative benefits

of prune juice and bran flakes.

Please drink four glasses of

prune juice before retiring on Tuesday

and report to our offices

first thing Wednesday morning

for the run-offs.

It should be a moving experience.

33. The Only Difference

Another metaphor for a business operation in difficult straits is that of a sinking ship. In this text from Sheboygan, Wisconsin, in 1988, the comparison is specifically made to the *Titanic*, one of the worst marine disasters of this century. The *Titanic*, a British steamer thought to be unsinkable, struck an iceberg on the night of April 14, 1912, during its first trip from England to the United States. Approximately fifteen hundred persons lost their lives in the tragedy, blamed in part on insufficient lifeboats.

The implication of the sign is that the state of the office in which it appears is even worse than the plight of the ill-fated *Titanic*. At least the poor souls on the ship had music.

THE ONLY
DIFFERENCE
BETWEEN THIS
PLACE
AND THE
TITANIC
IS THEY HAD A
BAND

34. Tell Me Again

No matter how unpleasant an office atmosphere may be, there is inevitably someone to remind one of the alternative, that is, unemployment. The following text was collected from an office in Sproul Hall, one of the principal administration buildings on the University of California, Berkeley, campus in 1988. The comment is clearly tongue-in-cheek.

The second version, collected in Virginia in May 1990, is accompanied by a cartoon figure which underscores the irony of the feigned expression of good fortune.

Tell me again how lucky I am to work here . . .

I keep forgetting

Never Try to Teach a Pig to Sing

PLEASE LORD, *TELL ME* AGAIN HOW LUCKY I AM TO BE WORKING HERE.

35. Of Course I Want It Today

Anyone who has worked in an office has encountered the unreasonable requester. He waits until the very last minute to make his request and then becomes angry when he does not receive instant service. The first version was collected in a federal government office in San Francisco in 1976. The second version was collected in a government research installation near Knoxville, Tennessee, in 1977. The third version was collected in the Inter-Library Loan office in the main library of the University of California, Berkeley, in 1976.

"OF COURSE I WANT IT TODAY!
IF I WANTED IT TOMORROW
I'D GIVE IT TO YOU TOMORROW."

Never Try to Teach a Pig to Sing

"OF COURSE I WANT IT TODAY!
IF I WANTED IT TOMORROW
I'D GIVE IT TO YOU TOMORROW!

OF COURSE I *want* it TODAY!
If I wanted it Tomorrow
I'd order it Tomorrow!

36. Poor Planning

No employee likes having to respond to pressure caused by a fellow employee's unreasonable demands. The following item from Sacramento in 1988 constitutes a protest against such a demand. For two English versions, see OHB, 45 and RIF, 147.

POOR PLANNING ON YOUR PART DOES NOT CONSTITUTE AN EMERGENCY ON MY PART!!

37. Proper Planning

Some of the anxiety connected with office work can be alleviated by thoughtful planning. In a society governed by an efficiency ethic, advance preparation is highly valued. The following alliterative slogan collected in Tennessee in 1977 expresses this philosophy.

PROPER PLANNING

PREVENTS

PISS-POOR PERFORMANCE

38. Plan Ahead

It is not enough just to make a viable plan. The plan must be made well in advance of the anticipated activity. The following text from New Baltimore, Michigan, in 1981 but dating back to at least 1973 makes the point with a biblical allusion.

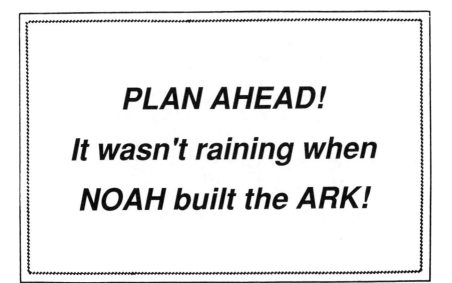

PLAN AHEAD!
It wasn't raining when
NOAH built the ARK!

39. All Skill Is in Vain

The German in this item is not pseudo-German, but the proverb may be. The sentiment, however, is accurate insofar as adverse circumstances may negate talent and effort. It was collected in southern California in 1976.

Alle künst ist unsunst
wenn ein engel auf
das zündloch brunst.*

*All skill is in vain if an angel pisses in the flintlock of your musket.

40. No Amount of Planning

Planning alone does not ensure success. As with life generally, it never hurts to have good fortune. The difficulty is that one cannot always count on being lucky. Also someone who succeeds primarily because of good luck rather than ability is likely to be the object of both envy and resentment. The following text from Foster City, California, in 1986, however, gives fatalistic recognition of the part luck sometimes plays in the workplace.

NO AMOUNT OF PLANNING WILL EVER REPLACE DUMB LUCK

41. Christmas Has Been Cancelled

Management is sometimes perceived as cruel and heartless insofar as it seems to place the work schedule above all—including national holidays and vacations. Christmas despite being as much a secular as a religious holiday is almost sacred in American culture. Not only is the Christmas vacation entirely eliminated in the following text, but the language of the directive displays an all-too-typical peremptory style. No explanation is deemed necessary and therefore none is offered.

It should also be noted that mandating a calendrical shift from December 25th to Easter eliminates by fiat the winter months, the slowest part of the business year for some firms. The proclamation hints at an abridgment of the entire life cycle in that Christmas, the time of the celebration of Christ's birth is omitted, and one is ordered to move immediately to the time of the commemoration of Christ's death by crucifixion. This text was collected in Torrance, California, in 1988.

Christmas has been Cancelled

go directly to dyeing eggs!

42. The Floggings Will Continue

Some employers recognize that low morale in the workplace can be detrimental to business success. The question is what action should be taken to improve morale. Normally, a carrot is used rather than a stick, that is, a policy of offering workers a positive incentive rather than a punishment might be instituted. In the following text collected from a mechanic at United Airlines at Los Angeles in 1988, the latter course is taken. The flowery old-fashioned script as well as the archaic word "floggings" enhance the irony of such an ill-advised and self-defeating management procedure.

43. When You Throw a Little Dirt

There are other forms of self-defeating activities. A person who attempts to malign a co-worker may find that he himself is adversely affected by this effort. Similarly, a politician who engages in a "dirty tricks" campaign may expose himself to the same risks as the general public may indicate its disapproval of such tactics at the ballot box. The wisdom contained in this item from Dublin, California, in 1980, is sometimes couched in different verbiage. For example, a proverb current in Berkeley in the 1960s was: "Mud thrown is ground lost."

When you throw

a little dirt . . .

You usually lose

a little ground.

44. Old Age and Treachery

While one may indignantly condemn "dirty tricks," it is also true that underhanded methods sometimes succeed. The combination of savvy gained from long years of experience with craft and wiliness may sometimes prevail over talented novices. The following aphorism from the Bay Area in 1980, however, runs counter to the fairy-tale norms in which the youngest/best motif typically triumphs. In American culture with its emphasis upon youth, it is somewhat surprising to find old age victorious. Presumably it is only with the aid of unethical behavior that youth can be thwarted. For another version, see YD [139].

Old Age and Treachery

Will Overcome

Youth and Skill

45. Use Your Head

Two traditional pieces of advice are combined in the following text collected in Berkeley in 1981. "Use your head" is a standard admonition suggesting that a person think carefully about a proposed course of action. "It's the little things that count" is a somewhat saccharine suggestion that one should take pride in minor details or small accomplishments (instead of reaching major goals). The juxtaposition of these two produces a third tradition, that of a "pinhead," or a brainless person.

Use your head
it's the little things
that count

46. I Work Better Under Pressure!!

While nearly everyone complains about having to work under the pressure of deadlines, the fact is that most people need the structure of circumscribed time limits in order to complete assignments. Cramming for examinations in school or so-called "crash projects," which are typically carried out "under the gun," illustrate this process. Would students study hard if there were no exams? Would projects be completed if there were no deadlines? The following item collected from a mechanic employed by United Airlines in Los Angeles is a grudging admission of the necessity for such structure. At the same time, there is more than a hint of bravado insofar as the put-upon employee almost dares the boss to clamp down even more. For an English version, see OHB, 51.

"GO AHEAD, YOU SON-OF-A-BITCH, GIVE IT A TURN! I WORK BETTER UNDER PRESSURE!!"

47. Your Rush Job

Part of the pressure in the workplace comes from last-minute deadlines for projects. Sometimes, in a given office, there may even be competing priorities. Occasionally, an employee may become confused about which job takes precedence over other demands. The following text from New Baltimore, Michigan, in 1981 reflects such an employee's bewilderment. For a version published in England, see RJ, 21.

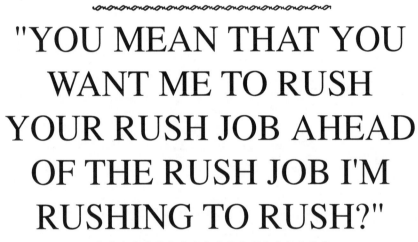

"YOU MEAN THAT YOU WANT ME TO RUSH YOUR RUSH JOB AHEAD OF THE RUSH JOB I'M RUSHING TO RUSH?"

48. As Soon as the Rush Is Over

Much of the strain in an office is mental. In some businesses, the degree of pressure varies with seasons or occasions. At such times, individuals may despair of meeting a deadline or surviving the crisis of the moment. In the following notice, the normally dreaded nervous breakdown is facetiously perceived as a reward for hard work. It is not easy to make fun of mental illness, but surely such fun may help avoid such illness by relieving stress.

The text was collected in Fishersville, Virginia, in 1989 and produced with computer graphics. For two additional versions, see UFFC-TB, 6–7; for English versions, see YWIW [108], TCB 59.

AS SOON AS THE RUSH IS OVER, I'M GOING TO HAVE A NERVOUS BREAKDOWN; I WORKED FOR IT, I DESERVE IT, and NOBODY CAN DEPRIVE ME OF IT !

49. We Welcome Your Problems

Customer service departments are supposed to receive complaints courteously. Sometimes, the courtesy is extended through gritted teeth as the department representative tries hard to remember the motto that "the customer is always right." The first version was collected in Costa Mesa, California, in 1976 while the second was collected in Maryland in 1978. The two versions show contrasting attitudes toward customer complaints: hostility and indifference. The variation in both text and cartoon figure is striking.

WE WELCOME YOUR PROBLEMS WITH ENTHUSIASM

WE GREET YOUR PROBLEM WITH ENTHUSIASM

50. We Welcome Advice

Many offices have suggestion boxes where employees are encouraged to offer advice and criticism. Some companies have even offered cash prizes to reward suggestions for money or time saving improvements. On the other hand, few management personnel can tolerate the implicit criticism inherent in most suggestions. In the vast majority of instances, the suggestions are filed and forgotten. The following notice collected in the University of California Lockshop in Berkeley in 1978 indicates the usual fate of suggestions. For another version, see YD [82].

We welcome Advice and Criticism. . . .

and Always <u>rush</u> Them through

the Proper Channels............

(One flush usually does it!)

51. This Office Is Open

Complaint departments may exist, but complaints are rarely welcome. The following facetious announcement was collected at the Community Development Agency of the city of Los Angeles in 1983.

THIS OFFICE IS OPEN
FOR ANY PROBLEM –
BUT PLEASE DO NOT
COME IN UNLESS YOU
HAVE A SOLUTION

52. Employees' Cooperation

If there are facetious invitations to employees to register complaints, there are also facetious complaints and smart aleck responses to complaints. Two standard American responses to unwelcome orders or requests are: "Go fly a kite!" "Go jump in the lake!" There are many other traditional retorts belonging to the same genre, e.g., "Go take a flying leap (at the moon, or at a rolling doughnut)," "Go take a long walk off a short pier," "Go piss up a rope," and "Go to hell." The following text from Berkeley in 1985 presumes a knowledge of the most common of these responses.

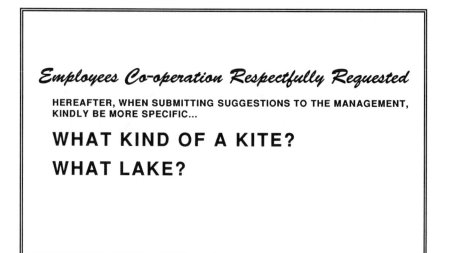

Employees Co-operation Respectfully Requested

HEREAFTER, WHEN SUBMITTING SUGGESTIONS TO THE MANAGEMENT, KINDLY BE MORE SPECIFIC...

WHAT KIND OF A KITE?

WHAT LAKE?

Never Try to Teach a Pig to Sing

53. Suppose We Refund Your Money

Supposedly "the customer is always right," but from management's point of view, there are some customers who are never satisfied. For those individuals, no corrective action taken by management will suffice. The following text from a Woodward and Lothrop department store in Wheaton, Maryland, circa 1980, reveals management's attitude toward the perennially dissatisfied customer.

Suppose we refund your money, send you another one without charge, close the store, and have the manager shot. Would that be satisfactory?

54. Please Don't Ask for Information

There are companies that maintain information booths for new clients in order to direct them to the appropriate floor, section, or office. The personnel who man such booths are not necessarily senior employees. While they may be able to give simple directions to locations, they may not be knowledgeable about specific technical details of a company's operation or products. The following item from New York City in 1984, presumably posted at or near an information booth, comments on this. It may also serve to put a prospective customer in a good mood.

The second item, which was also collected in New York City, though in 1989, offers a different excuse for the ignorance of office personnel. It is a commentary of the stereotypic distinction between brains and beauty. The American folk stereotype links beauty and stupidity while associating homeliness with brains. In this case, the monkey figure connotes neither intelligence nor good looks.

PLEASE, DON'T ASK FOR INFORMATION IF WE KNEW ANYTHING, WE WOULDN'T BE HERE

55. Answers Price List

Some individuals when asked a question are embarrassed to admit they don't know the answer. So rather than admit their ignorance, they make up something. The following item from Berkeley in 1988 recognizes the fact that answers are not always correct. It also suggests that one has to pay for reliable information. For another version, see YD [46]. For an English version, see RJ, 36.

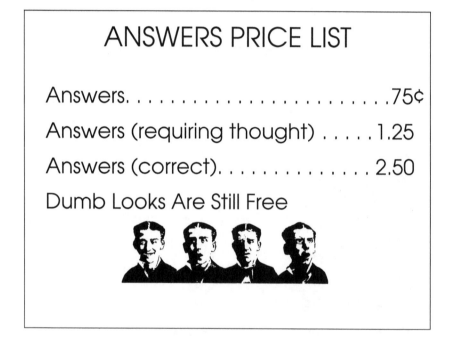

ANSWERS PRICE LIST

Answers. . . . . .75¢

Answers (requiring thought) 1.25

Answers (correct). 2.50

Dumb Looks Are Still Free

56. Labor Rates

Many workers prefer the customer to be absent when a job is undertaken. A customer who wishes to oversee the completion of a job may make inappropriate suggestions or may simply make the worker nervous. Also, if a worker is obliged to stop every so often to answer unwelcome questions or to explain a procedure, the job may take much longer. To discourage kibitzers, the following sign collected from the Community Development Agency of the City of Los Angeles in 1983 indicates the cost of observing the worker in action. A second version from Lancashire, England, in 1978, places the work venue in a garage. For another version, see YD [155]; for another English version, see RIF, 150.

Normal . . . . $12.50 per hour
If you wait . . . . . . 15.00 per hour
If you watch . . . . . 20.00 per hour
If you help . . . . . . 30.00 per hour

LABOUR RATE

AT THIS GARAGE IS AS FOLLOWS

PER HOUR

MINIMUM RATE	£ 3.50
CUSTOMERS WATCHING	£ 4.50
CUSTOMERS GIVING ADVICE	£ 6.00
CUSTOMERS HELPING	£ 10.00

57. Just When I Knew All the Answers

The fast pace of technological change in the business world tends to create instant obsolescence. Yesterday's expertise is inadequate to answer the pressing questions of today. The following text from the Bay Area in the 1980s bemoans this exasperating situation.

"Just when I knew all the answers, they changed all the questions."

58. When I'm Right

No matter how many times an individual may perform well, it is typically his mistakes which tend to be remembered. Shakespeare remarked on this tendency in Marc Antony's celebrated funeral oration in *Julius Caesar* (III, ii, 81–82): "The evil that men do lives after them; The good is oft interred with their bones." The folk agree. The following text was collected in Tennessee in 1977.

WHEN I'M RIGHT,
NO ONE REMEMBERS

WHEN I'M WRONG,
NO ONE FORGETS

59. If We Can't Fix It

One of the most outrageous pieces of folk braggadocio was collected in 1978 in the University of California, Berkeley, Lockshop which offers repair and maintenance services for Dwinelle Hall, a very large classroom and office complex. It was on an oversize piece of paper, approximately eight inches in height and two feet in width. The message effectively denied the possibility of failure. It is also an obvious play on the modern American proverb: "If it ain't broke, don't fix it."

IF WE CAN'T FIX IT

IT AINT **BUSTED**

60. Security Is Like Virginity

The following notice was found posted behind a desk in a security building at Fort Bragg, North Carolina, in 1965.

> Security is like virginity—once compromised, it's lost forever.

Similar uses of sexual metaphors to describe life could be cited. For example, a well-known text collected in the women's restroom in Barrows Hall at the University of California, Berkeley, in 1971 (but also found in oral tradition) goes as follows:

> Life is like a penis. When it's soft, you can't beat it and when it's hard, you get fucked.

Not all such comparisons are sexual in nature. The following text was collected in Oakland in 1977:

> Some minds are like concrete—all mixed up and permanently set.

It should be noted, however, that most graffiti do not enter the notices, memoranda, and other paperwork forms encountered in xerographic tradition. A graffito which becomes enshrined in a wall plaque is the exception rather than the rule.

61. Be Sure to Work Eight Hours

The standard workday involves a period of eight hours, e.g., nine to five. Hospital, factory, and other round-the-clock operations may divide the day into three eight-hour shifts: regular (8 to 4), swing (4 to midnight), and graveyard (midnight to 8) or variations thereof. If one considers that eight hours of every working day is spent at one's job, and eight hours are devoted to sleep, this leaves only eight hours for everything else. If a person tries to expand the time for personal activities at the expense of the normal time set aside for sleep, he or she may find himself dozing off at work. The following text from Buffalo in 1982 comments on this practice with the implicit warning that one has an obligation to stay alert on the job.

Be Sure to Work 8 Hours
and Sleep 8 Hours . . .

but not the same 8 hours!

62. A Day Off

The distinction between time spent at work and time spent at play is a critical one in American culture. There are periods of time interspersed during the workday, such as coffee breaks and lunchtime, which may or may not technically count as part of the workday. There are also holidays—some national, some local—which may or may not be recognized by individual companies. The calculation of work-time is therefore subject to considerable variation. The following item utilizing statistical reasoning is a commentary on the calculation of vacation from work. It was collected from a sales clerk in a Bullocks Department store in downtown Los Angeles in 1989. For English versions, see OHB, 18 and RIF, 46.

"A DAY OFF"

So you want the day off. Let's take a look at what you are asking for.

There are 365 days per year available for work. There are 52 weeks per year in which you already have two days off per week, leaving 261 days available for work. Since you spend 16 hours each day away from work, you have used up 170 days, leaving only 91 days available. You spend 30 minutes each day on coffee break that accounts for 23 days each year, leaving only 68 days available. With a one hour lunch period each day, you have used up another 46 days, leaving only 22 days available for work. You normally spend 2 days per year on sick leave. This leaves you only 20 days available for work. We are off for 5 holidays per year, so your available working time is down to 15 days. We generously give you 14 days vacation per year which leaves only 1 day available for work and I'll be damned if you're going to take that day off!!!!

63. I'm Tired

A similar use of statistics is used to eliminate nearly the entire population of the United States from the work force. The following text was collected from a Glendale Federal Savings bank in Fullerton, California, in 1988. However, the figure of 200 million for the population of the U.S. suggests an earlier date. Other versions (usually entitled "Are You Tired?") have attempted to update the statistics, e.g., giving the U.S. population as 220 million. For English versions, see YWIW [102] and TCB, 12. For a Swedish version, see MF, 29.

I'M TIRED

Yes, I'm tired. For several years I've been blaming it on middleage, iron poor blood, lack of vitamins, air pollution, water pollution, saccharin, obesity, dieting, under-arm odor, yellow wax build-up, and a dozen other maladies that make you wonder if life is really worth living.

But now I find out, tain't that.

I'm tired because I'm overworked.

The population of this country is 200 million. Eighty-four million are retired. That leaves 116 million to do the work. There are 75 million in school, which leaves 41 million to do the work. Of this total, there are 22 million employed by the government.

That leaves 19 million to do the work.

Four million are in the Armed forces, which leaves 15 million to do the work. Take from that total the 14,800,000 people who work for State and City Government and that leaves 200,000 to do the work. There are 188,000 in hospitals, so that leaves 12,000 to do the work.

Now, there are 11,998 people in prisons. That leaves just two people to do the work. You and me. And you're sitting there reading this. No wonder I'm Tired.

–Anonymous–

64. This Life Is a Test

Radio and television stations test emergency broadcast facilities periodically. Usually these tests are preceded by an announcement stating that what follows is merely a test. The announcement also includes a closing reminder that if it had been an actual emergency, specific instructions would have been issued. The following item collected in Berkeley in 1988 is a parody of such emergency tests. The philosophical implication is that one's life is only a futile exercise that doesn't really count.

This life is a test—it is only a test. If it had been an actual life, you would have received further instructions on where to go and what to do.

Never Try to Teach a Pig to Sing

65. No Physical Fitness Program

One of the problems of modern urban America is the lack of physical activity in so many jobs. As more and more individuals find themselves in a sedentary work position, such as sitting in front of a computer or word processor or behind a desk, there has been an increasing concern for the possible effects of such work habits on the physical well-being of employees. Some individuals have taken up jogging during the lunch break. Selected business firms have sought to encourage employees desirous of participating in such exercise programs by installing "changing rooms" (to change into or out of running garb), showers, or in some instances full-fledged gymnasium facilities containing exercise equipment.

The following item from the Poultry Science Lab at the University of California, Davis, in 1988, is a commentary on physical fitness programs. Through a series of common metaphors (which are literalized), it is claimed that employees get plenty of physical exercise. For another version, see YD [103]; for an English version, see RIF, 146.

NOTICE

THIS PLACE REQUIRES NO PHYSICAL FITNESS PROGRAM.
EVERYONE GETS ENOUGH EXERCISE
JUMPING TO CONCLUSIONS,
FLYING OFF THE HANDLE,
RUNNING DOWN THE BOSS,
KNIFING FRIENDS IN THE BACK,
DODGING RESPONSIBILITY
AND
PUSHING THEIR LUCK!

66. Quitting Time

The use of "dead" as an adjective to describe lazy or inactive workers is evidently not too extreme a term. The phrase "dead-wood" suggests both stagnation and incompetence. The issue is the relationship between one's work and one's life. For some individuals, one's work is one's life, but for others, work is a necessary evil endured to permit one to live. For the latter, life is at home or, at any rate, outside the office. Leisure or pleasure occurs only after leaving work. The conception of clock-watchers in American culture refers to people who watch the clock ticking off the minutes until the workday is done.

The following item was collected at a telephone company office in New Hampshire in mid-1977. It should be noted that the folk have appropriated the character of Snoopy from the "Peanuts" comic strip of Charles Schulz. For another version, see YD [107]; for an English version entitled "Resurrection," see TCB, 66. (For another illustration of the death metaphor in an office setting, see "Instructions on Death of Employees" in WH, 85–86.)

PEOPLE WHO BELIEVE THAT THE DEAD

NEVER COME BACK TO LIFE ....

SHOULD BE HERE AT QUITTING TIME !

"CHARGE !!"

MA-BELL

Never Try to Teach a Pig to Sing

67. In Case of Fire

Another commentary on the surge of activity which is to be found at the end of the workday appears in the following text collected from a bulletin board at the Computer Science and Applied Mathematics Division of the Lawrence Berkeley Laboratory in 1982.

IN CASE OF FIRE

SIMPLY FLEE BUILDING WITH

THE SAME RECKLESS ABANDON

THAT OCCURS EACH DAY AT

QUITTING TIME.

68. This Property Protected

After the employees have left the workplace, the premises must be locked and made secure. There may be a watchman or some kind of electronic surveillance or alarm system. In a few cases, guard dogs may be employed. Typically, signs are posted indicating the presence of dogs or a security system.

The following item from Fishersville, Virginia, in 1989, parodies building security signs. Pitbulls have been at the center of some media controversy in the United States because of their sometimes fierce behavior (and their utilization in illegal dogfights). Some communities have sought to ban pitbull ownership, usually after a child has been severely bitten. In this parody, we see once again the folk fear of the dread disease AIDS, which has been fancifully linked with what is normally construed as a dangerous dog.

This Property
Protected By

PITBULL

with

AIDS

Kopy Kat Security Systems

69. Be Tolerant

In any healthy office or business, there is bound to be a diversity of opinion. Sometimes, situations demand that one view rather than another prevail so that the work of the office can go on. Ideally, one should be tolerant of competing perspectives, but in reality it is often difficult to concede the merit of alternative positions. The following text from Honeywell in Silverdale, Washington, in 1979 initially feigns tolerance.

Be tolerant of those who disagree with you; after all, they have a right to their stupid opinions.

70. People Who Think
They Know Everything

One reason why it is sometimes difficult to respect the opinions of others is that these other opinions are held by know-it-alls. The question of what happens when two know-it-alls clash is the subject of the following item collected from the University Extension building in Berkeley in 1978. A second version from Berkeley in 1981 demonstrates considerable variation. For an English version, see RIF, 145.

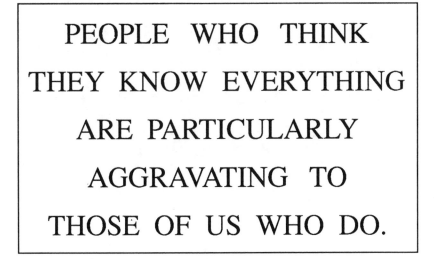

PEOPLE WHO THINK
THEY KNOW EVERYTHING
ARE PARTICULARLY
AGGRAVATING TO
THOSE OF US WHO DO.

NOTICE

THOSE OF YOU WHO THINK YOU KNOW IT ALL REALLY PISS OFF THOSE OF US WHO DO!!

Never Try to Teach a Pig to Sing

71. Nobody Is Perfect

The following popular notice is a mocking admission that form may be more important than substance. One may be prejudiced (in the sense of making a pre-judgment) but one must give the appearance of "giving the guilty bastard a fair trial." This text was collected in San Francisco in 1975. It is frequently found in elaborately printed commercial versions as well as in a metal plaque format. For two other versions, see UFFC-TB, 9–10; for an English version, see RIF, 32.

Nobody Is Perfect

Each one of us is a mixture of good qualities and some perhaps not-so-good qualities. In considering our fellow man we should remember his good qualities and realize that his faults only prove that he is, after all, a human being. We should refrain from making harsh judgement of a person just because he happens to be a dirty, rotten, no-good son-of-a-bitch!

When Things Go Wrong

Despite the advantages of modern technolgy and sophisticated office management, errors and mistakes inevitably crop up with regularity. The human capacity for misjudgment can neither be underestimated nor avoided. The folk have clearly recognized this in numerous examples of commentary on the subject.

Generally speaking, in American culture one finds a great deal of sympathy for individuals who make mistakes. Americans tend to root for unpromising heroes and underdogs; they prefer to pardon rather than punish criminals. Of course, not all mistakes are equally forgivable. Doctors, lawyers, and other professionals have been forced to purchase expensive malpractice insurance while engineers and architects purchase "errors and omissions" insurance. As long as ships sink, planes crash, factories explode, and bridges collapse, we will continue to live in an imperfect world.

One should keep in mind that catastrohes and human foibles very often inspire humor. From pratfalls to slips of the tongue, people never seem to tire of watching others embarrass themselves by making mistakes. Whole television programs are devoted to presenting series of bloopers and gaffs. Perhaps it is all a means of feeling superior. One can be smug insofar as the mistake was made by someone else.

The individual who makes a serious mistake may not be so amused. Still, to the extent that all of us err, we cannot help but recognize that failure of some kind is a natural part of the universal human condition.

72. Don't Quit

One of the few things worse than making a bad mistake is to give up or to be a quitter because of it. Adversity is to be overcome. One should learn from one's mistakes. Among the qualities needed to succeed in the face of difficulty is persistence, the ability to see a problem through.

The following hortatory folk poem from Ohio in 1981 articulates this philosophy. A second version from Berkeley in 1983 contains only the first stanza of the poem, but its tone is quite different, as signaled by the last lines and the accompanying gesture made by the cartoon figure, which is a folk appropriation of Walt Disney's celebrated Mickey Mouse. Here the implication is that a person's problems are his or her own and that no one else really cares. A third exemplar, from Walnut Creek, California, 1988, reveals the same cartoon figure attached to a completely different text, this time complaining about someone who has parked his car poorly. For a Danish version, see CS 92. For an English parallel to the first stanza of the first version, see RIF, 40. A fourth item, collected in Chicago in 1982, confirms the independence of texts and figures. The collecting context of this latter item is of interest because it was found stuck behind a windshield wiper on a car parked in the Cook County criminal court lot. (For another version of the fourth item, see YD [83]; for a different xerographic item concerned with poor parking, see WY, 53.)

DON'T QUIT

When things go wrong, as they sometimes will,
When the road you are trudging is all uphill,
When the funds are low and the debts are high,
And you want to smile, but you have to sigh,
When care is pressing you down a bit,
Rest, if you must, BUT DON'T QUIT.

Life is queer with its twists and turns,
As every one of us sometimes learns,
And many a fellow turns about,
When he might have won, had he stuck it out.
Don't "give up," though the pace seems slow,
YOU MAY SUCCEED WITH ANOTHER BLOW.

Often the goal is nearer than
it seems to a faint and faltering man,
Often the struggler has given up,
when he might have captured the Victor's Cup,
And he learned too late when the night came
    down
HOW CLOSE HE WAS
    TO THE GOLDEN CROWN.

Success is failure turned inside out,
The silver tint of the clouds of doubt,
And you never can tell how close you are,
It may be near when it seems so far,
So stick to the fight when you're hardest hit,
IT'S WHEN THINGS SEEM WORSE THAT
    YOU
        MUST NOT QUIT!

(Author Unknown)

WHEN THINGS GO WRONG
AS THEY USUALLY WILL,
AND YOUR DAILY ROAD
SEEMS ALL UPHILL
WHEN FUNDS ARE LOW
AND DEBTS ARE HIGH
WHEN YOU TRY TO SMILE
BUT CAN ONLY CRY
AND YOU REALLY FEEL
YOU'D LIKE TO QUIT
DON'T RUN TO ME:
I DON'T GIVE A SHIT.

When Things Go Wrong

73. Oh No!

On occasion an alert secretary or subordinate can catch an error made by the boss. On the other hand, workers may be understandably reluctant to change any directive from above without express permission to do so. In the case where an employee has carried out instructions to the letter, the boss may have to take the blame for his own mistake. The first version of the following item was collected in San Francisco in 1980. The second version was collected from the computerized control room of the Kaiser Cement plant located in Permanente, California, in June 1989. The anguished face in the first item seems related to the figure found in the second version of item 34 above.

OH NO!

YOU'VE DONE IT JUST LIKE I TOLD YOU!!!

74. Lonesome?

Tolerance for mistakes varies from office to office. In some instances, an employee might be given a second chance. The ultimate sanction for error is termination. The following text from Berkeley in 1981 seems to follow the format of an advertising promotion, e.g., for a travel agency or military recruitment. For another version, see YD [110]; for English versions, see OHB, 4 and TCB, 56.

LONESOME?

LIKE TO MEET PEOPLE?

LIKE A CHANGE?

LIKE EXCITEMENT?

LIKE A NEW JOB?

JUST SCREW UP

ONE MORE TIME

75. What Went Wrong

When a mistake is made, no one wants to accept blame. The following text from the Nestlé coffee manufacturing plant in Ripon, California, in 1988 shows how anonymity may protect the perpetrator. Other versions of this item are entitled "Who Dunnit" and "A Little Story." For an English version, see RIF, 123.

WHAT WENT WRONG

This is the story of four people
Everybody, Somebody, Anybody, Nobody.
There was an important job to be done
And Everybody was sure that Somebody would
    do it.
Anybody could have done it but Nobody did it.
Somebody got angry because it was Everybody's
    job.
Everybody thought Somebody would do it
But Nobody asked.
It ended up that the job was not done
And Everybody blamed Somebody
When actually Nobody asked Anybody.

Never Try to Teach a Pig to Sing

76. God, I Love This Place

One reason why some things don't get accomplished in an office is that employees may lack motivation or energy. A woman who takes her shoes off and rests on her typewriter is surely comfortable in her work environment. The wilting plant is evidently in sympathy with the mood of the secretary. Her statement of devotion to the office is in direct contradiction with the piles of work sitting on the floor awaiting her attention.

The first version is from Foster City, California, 1986. A second version, collected in a hospital blood-testing laboratory in Berkeley in 1989, includes a more extensive text. A third version from Fishersville, Virginia, in 1989 is clearly related to the second version, but it bears a different title and has a different drawing. For another version with an elephant behind a desk, see YD [63]; for an English version, see RIF, 149.

GOD I LOVE THIS PLACE....

Please be patient, I only work here
   because I am too old
   for a paper route —
   too young for social security
& too tired to have an affair

PLEASE BE PATIENT...

... I ONLY WORK HERE BECAUSE—
I'M TOO OLD FOR A PAPER ROUTE,
TOO YOUNG FOR SOCIAL SECURITY,
AND TOO TIRED TO HAVE AN AFFAIR!

77. I'm 51 Percent Sweetheart

A good secretary has to talk a fine line between being helpful to prospective clients and fellow employees and being hard-nosed with respect to protecting her boss and her own time from nuisance visitors and requests. The fine line need not be exactly 50/50 as is illustrated in the following item from Fishersville, Virginia, in 1989. A second version, collected from a trucking company in Eureka, California, in November 1989, shows variation in both figure and the relatively short caption.

I'M
51% SWEETHEART
AND
49% BITCH
SO DON'T PUSH IT!!!

I'M
51% SWEETHEART
49% BITCH
DON'T PUSH IT!

78. Before Work/After Work

The frustration level increases as the day goes on. In the early morning, personnel are calm and collected. By the end of the workday, the same individuals are frazzled. The fat cat character resembles Garfield the Cat, a well-known cartoon figure created by Jim Davis. The second figure in the item is the same as that found in the definition of "Stress" (see item 17 above). The following item was collected in Oakland in 1988.

The second item, collected in Walnut Creek, California, in July 1990, also contrasts "before" and "after." In this case, it is the end of the day which provides the point of departure. The next morning reveals ugly reality. A woman—a crown suggests a princess or queen—may see herself or be seen by others as beautiful thanks to dim light, thick smoke, and the effects of alcohol. The vision may change drastically with the morning light. The reader is invited to compare the two images by turning the item upside down. (For other xerographic items utilizing the same kind of double image, see IK, 110 and WY, 58.)

BEFORE
WORK

AFTER
WORK

Never Try to Teach a Pig to Sing

CLOSING TIME AT THE BAR

NEXT MORNING REALITY

79. When I Woke Up This Morning

An individual under stress in an office may become irritated by a particular circumstance or person. The disheveled appearance of the woman in the following item from the Public Information Office of the City of Oakland in 1982 suggests that she is in such a state. The expression "to get on my nerves" refers to a person greatly upset by a specific person or event. The statement that the woman in the cartoon has only one nerve shows that she is at the end of her rope, that all of her other nerves have become numb from the shocks of previous workdays.

When I woke up this morning
I had one nerve left,
...And now you're getting on it!

Never Try to Teach a Pig to Sing

80. So You Think You Got Troubles

There are other illustrations of hitting a nerve. The folk cartoon of a cow stepping on her udder goes back at least to the early 1940s. The version presented below was collected in San Francisco at that time. (A version almost identical was collected in Indiana in 1976.) Legman alludes to a version from New York City in 1950 in his discussion of anti-breast fetishism. See NLM, 365.

So you think you got troubles?

81. Doing the Job Alone

Instead of a huge list of troubles, we find an elaborate description of just one single mishap. The following account of a bricklayer's misadventure has various titles, e.g., "Poor Planning," "It's the Truth," and "An Incredible-But Apparently? True 'On-the-Job' Accident Report." Several versions indicate that the bricklayer was from Barbados and that the letter allegedly appeared in the *Manchester Guardian*. In one version, the letter-writer is a mechanic working in a mill rather than a bricklayer.

Frequently, in order to justify absence from a job or to request workman's compensation for job-related injuries, one is required to provide adequate explanation to one's employer or one's insurance company. The text below from Buffalo in 1980 is a parody of such an explanation. This item is also found in oral tradition and as a folksong. For a version in print, see James T. Cleland, *Preaching to Be Understood* (New York: Abingdon Press, 1965), pp. 115–16.

DOING THE JOB ALONE

DEAR SIR:

I AM WRITING IN RESPONSE TO YOUR REQUEST FOR
MORE INFORMATION CONCERNING BLOCK #11 ON THE
INSURANCE FORM WHICH ASKS FOR "CAUSE OF IN-
JURIES" WHEREIN I PUT "TRYING TO DO THE JOB
ALONE." YOU SAID YOU NEEDED MORE INFORMATION
SO I TRUST THE FOLLOWING WILL BE SUFFICIENT.

I AM A BRICKLAYER BY TRADE AND ON THE DATE OF
INJURIES I WAS WORKING ALONE LAYING BRICK
AROUND THE TOP OF A FOUR-STORY BUILDING WHEN I
REALIZED THAT I HAD ABOUT 500 POUNDS OF BRICK
LEFT OVER. RATHER THAN CARRY THE BRICKS DOWN
BY HAND, I DECIDED TO PUT THEM INTO A BARREL
AND LOWER THEM BY A PULLEY WHICH WAS FASTENED
TO THE TOP OF THE BUILDING. I SECURED THE END OF
THE ROPE AT GROUND LEVEL AND WENT UP TO THE
TOP OF THE BUILDING AND LOADED THE BRICKS INTO
THE BARREL AND SWUNG THE BARREL OUT WITH THE
BRICKS IN IT. I THEN WENT DOWN AND UNTIED THE
ROPE, HOLDING IT SECURELY TO INSURE THE SLOW
DESCENT OF THE BARREL.

AS YOU WILL NOTE ON BLOCK #6 OF THE INSURANCE FORM, I WEIGH 195 POUNDS. DUE TO MY SHOCK AT BEING JERKED OFF THE GROUND SO SWIFTLY, I LOST MY PRESENCE OF MIND AND FORGOT TO LET GO OF THE ROPE. BETWEEN THE SECOND AND THIRD FLOORS I MET THE BARREL COMING DOWN. THIS ACCOUNTS FOR THE BRUISES AND LACERATIONS ON MY UPPER BODY.

REGAINING MY PRESENCE OF MIND, I HELD TIGHTLY TO THE ROPE AND PROCEEDED RAPIDLY UP THE SIDE OF THE BUILDING, NOT STOPPING UNTIL MY RIGHT HAND WAS JAMMED IN THE PULLEY. THIS ACCOUNTS FOR THE BROKEN THUMB.

DESPITE THE PAIN, I RETAINED MY PRESENCE OF MIND AND HELD TIGHTLY TO THE ROPE. AT APPROXIMATELY THE SAME TIME, HOWEVER, THE BARREL OF BRICKS HIT THE GROUND AND THE BOTTOM FELL OUT OF THE BARREL. DEVOID OF THE WEIGHT OF THE BRICKS, THE BARREL NOW WEIGHED ABOUT 50 POUNDS. I AGAIN REFER YOU TO BLOCK #6 AND MY WEIGHT.

AS YOU WOULD GUESS, I BEGAN A RAPID DESCENT. IN THE VICINITY OF THE SECOND FLOOR I MET THE BARREL COMING UP. THIS EXPLAINS THE INJURIES TO MY LEGS AND LOWER BODY. SLOWED ONLY SLIGHTLY, I CONTINUED MY DESCENT, LANDING ON THE PILE OF BRICKS. FORTUNATELY, MY BACK WAS ONLY SPRAINED, AND THE INTERNAL INJURIES WERE MINIMAL.

I AM SORRY TO REPORT, HOWEVER, THAT AT THIS POINT, I FINALLY LOST MY PRESENCE OF MIND AND LET GO OF THE ROPE, AND AS YOU CAN IMAGINE, THE EMPTY BARREL CRASHED DOWN ON ME.

I TRUST THIS ANSWERS YOUR CONCERN. PLEASE KNOW THAT I AM FINISHED "TRYING TO DO THE JOB ALONE." HOW ABOUT YOU?

—ORIGINAL SOURCE UNKNOWN

82. The Revised Revision Revised

If there's one thing worse than writing reports, it is re-writing reports. In a large organization, many individuals may be involved in the chain of submission or transmission of a report. Each individual may have his or her own idea of what should be included in the report or how the subject matter could be better worded. In the following cartoon collected in Tennessee in 1977, a victim of countless requests for changes is subjected to yet another such request.

YOU mean YOU WANT the REVISED
REVISION of the ORIGINAL
REVISED REVISION
REVISED?

83. Dear Mr. Jefferson

Anyone who writes—students preparing term papers for instructors, office workers composing reports for superiors, authors submitting manuscripts for publication—faces the unpleasant prospect of editorial review. Sometimes the review focuses upon form and style rather than substance and may constitute nitpicking. The suggestions for revision can be so exasperating as to infuriate the original writer. One wonders whether any of the great writers of the past had to suffer the indignities of having their best efforts scrutinized by an overly zealous copy editor and if not, one cannot help but speculate what their final prose might have looked like had they been forced to endure such an agonizing process.

The following text from Berkeley in 1978 pretends to query Thomas Jefferson on the "Declaration of Independence."

July 20, 1776

Mr. Thomas Jefferson
Continental Congress
Independence Hall
Philadelphia, Pa.

Dear Mr. Jefferson:

We have read your "Declaration of Independence" with great interest. Certainly, it represents a considerable undertaking, and many of your statements do merit serious consideration. Unfortunately, the Declaration as a whole fails to meet recently adopted specifications for proposals to the Crown, so we must return the document to you for further refinement. The questions which follow might assist you in your process of revision.

1. In your opening paragraph you use the phrase "the Laws of Nature and Nature's God." What are these laws? In what way are they the criteria on which you base your central arguments? Please document with citations from the recent literature.

2. In the same paragraph you refer to the "opinions of mankind." Whose polling data are you using? Without specific evidence, it seems to us, the "opinions of mankind" are a matter of opinion.

3. You hold certain truths to be "self-evident." Could you please elaborate. If they are as evident as you claim, then it should not be difficult for you to locate the appropriate supporting statistics.

4. "Life, liberty, and the pursuit of happiness" seem to be the goals of your proposal. These are not measurable goals. If you were to say that "among these is the ability to sustain an average life expectancy in six of the 13 colonies for at least 55 years, and to enable all newspapers in the colonies to print news without outside interference, and to raise the average income of the colonists by 10 percent in the next 10 years," these would be measurable goals. Please clarify.

5. You state that "whenever any Form of Government becomes destructive of these ends, it is the Right of the People to alter or to abolish it, and to institute a new Government . . . . " Have you weighed this assertion against all the alternatives? Or is it predicated solely on the baser instincts?

6. Your description of the existing situation is quite extensive. Such a long list of grievances should precede the statement of goals, not follow it.

7. Your strategy for achieving your goal is not developed at all. You state that the colonies "ought to be Free and Independent States," and that they are "Absolved from All Allegiance to the British Crown." Who or what must they change? What resistance must you overcome to achieve the change? What specific steps will you take to overcome the resistance? How long will it take? We have found that a little foresight in these areas helps to prevent careless errors later on.

8. Who among the list of signatories will be responsible for implementing your strategy? Who conceived it? Who provided the theoretical research? Who will constitute the advisory committee? Please submit an organizational chart.

9. You must include an evaluation design. We have been requiring this since Queen Anne's War.

10. What impact will your program have? Your failure to include any assessment of this inspires little confidence in the long-range prospects of your undertaking.

11. Please submit a PERT diagram, an activity chart, and an itemized budget.

We hope that these comments prove useful in revising your "Declaration of Independence."

Best wishes,
Lord North

84. Four Score and Seven Years Ago

Even Abraham Lincoln's famed "Gettysburg Address" becomes just another composition, grist for the red pencil of a picky editor. This version was collected, appropriately enough, in Washington, D.C., in 1978. For a brief but very amusing rebuttal of a copy editor's inane suggestions for correction, see the "Publisher's Note" in T. E. Lawrence, *Revolt in the Desert* (Garden City: Garden City Publishing Company, 1926), pp. xii–xiv.

ARCHAIC
SAY EIGHTY-SEVEN

Too General!

FOUR SCORE AND SEVEN YEARS AGO OUR FATHERS BROUGHT FORTH ON THIS CONTINENT, A NEW NATION, CONCEIVED IN LIBERTY, AND DEDICATED TO THE PROPOSITION THAT ALL MEN ARE CREATED EQUAL.

How ABOUT THE WOMEN?

ENDURE WHAT? ELABORATE

NOW WE ARE ENGAGED IN A GREAT CIVIL WAR; TESTING WHETHER THAT NATION OR ANY NATION CONCEIVED AND SO DEDICATED, CAN LONG ENDURE. WE ARE MET ON A GREAT BATTLEFIELD OF THAT WAR. WE HAVE COME TO DEDICATE A PORTION OF THAT FIELD AS A FINAL RESTING PLACE FOR THOSE WHO HERE GAVE THEIR LIVES THAT THAT NATION MIGHT LIVE. IT IS ALTOGETHER FITTING AND PROPER THAT WE SHOULD DO THIS. BUT, IN A LARGER SENSE, WE CANNOT DEDICATE – WE CANNOT CONSECRATE – WE CANNOT HALLOW – THIS GROUND. THE BRAVE MEN, LIVING AND DEAD, WHO STRUGGLES HERE HAVE CONSECRATED IT, FAR ABOVE OUR POOR POWER TO ADD OR DETRACT. THE WORLD WILL LITTLE NOTE, NOR LONG REMEMBER, WHAT WE SAY HERE, BUT IT CAN NEVER FORGET WHAT THEY DID HERE. IT IS FOR US THE LIVING, RATHER, TO BE DEDICATED HERE TO THE UNFINISHED WORK WHICH THEY WHO FOUGHT HERE HAVE THUS FAR SO NOBLY ADVANCED. IT IS FOR US RATHER TO BE HERE DEDICATED TO THE GREAT TASK REMAINING BEFORE US THAT FROM THESE HONORED DEAD WE TAKE INCREASED DEVOTION TO THAT CAUSE FOR WHICH THEY GAVE THE LAST FULL MEASURE OF DEVOTION; THAT WE HERE HIGHLY RESOLVE THAT THESE DEAD SHALL NOT HAVE DIED IN VAIN; THAT THIS NATION UNDER GOD SHALL HAVE A NEW BIRTH OF FREEDOM; AND THAT GOVERNMENT OF THE PEOPLE. BY THE PEOPLE, FOR THE PEOPLE, SHALL NOT PERISH FROM THE EARTH.

WHAT WAR?

Double talk

Redundant

Say cemetery don't beat around the bush.

Statistics please HOW MANY OF EACH!

Then why say it? better omit.

Too ambiguous be specific.

BE MORE SPECIFIC, what is your PROGRAM

Advanced what?

Too much repetition.

This should END with A punch LINE!

HAS THIS BEEN COORDINATED WITH THE CHAPLAIN?

I don't think you have The idea at all! Better see me on this –

Never Try to Teach a Pig to Sing

85. All He Rites Is Buzniss

While businessmen are expected to speak and write reasonably well, it is sales in the final analysis which are of all-consuming importance. The American dream has always allowed for the self-made man who even without formal education could by dint of his own energy and initiative climb Horatio Alger-like to the top.

The following item was collected at a meeting of the American Iron and Steel Institute at the Duquesne Club in Pittsburgh, Pennsylvania, in April 1976. A second version, from Winnipeg, Cannada, in 1980, is entitled "Sel Not Spel" and demonstrates considerable variation. For a Swedish text, see MF, 46.

ALL HE RITES IS BUZNISS—A newly hired traveling salesman wrote his first sales report to the home office. It stunned company executives since it indicated the new man, Smith, was hopelessly illiterate. This is what he wrote:

"I SEEN THIS OUTFIT WHICH AIN'T NEVER BOT A DIMES WORTH OF NOTHIN FROM US AND I SOLE THEM A CUPLE A HUNRED TOUSAN DOLLARS OF GUDS. I AM NOW GOIN TO CHICAGOW—SMITH"

Before the sales manager could fire the illiterate salesman, along came another letter:

"I CUM HERE AND SOLE THEM HAFF A MILLYON—SMITH"

Before firing Smith, the sales manager decided to dump the problem in the lap of the company president.

The following morning, members of the home office sales staff saw the two letters posted on the bulletin board and this letter from the president tacked above:

"WE BEN SPENDIN TWO DAM MUCH TIME TRYING TO SPEL INSTEAD OF TRYIN TO SEL. LETS WACH THOES SALES. I WANT EVERYBODY SHOULD READ THESE LETTERS FROM SMITH WHO IS ON THE RODE DOING A GRATE JOB FOR US, AND YOU SHOULD GO OUT AND DO LIKE HE DONE."

SEL NOT SPEL

A newly hired traveling salesman wrote his first report to the home office. It stunned the brass in the sales department because it was obvious the new man was a blithering illiterate.

Here is what he wrote . . . .

Dere Bos—

I have seen this here outfit which ain't never bot a dimes worth of nothing from us and I sole them a cuple hunerd thousand dolars of guds.

I am now going to Chicawgo.

Before the illiterate could be given the heave-ho by the sales manager, this letter came from Chicago:

Dere Bos—

I cum hear to Chicawgo and sole them a haff a millyon.

Fearful if he did, and fearful if he didn't fire the illiterate, the sales manager dumped the problem in the lap of the president.

The following morning the ivory tower members were amazed to see the two letters posted on the bulletin board—and this memo from the president above:

TO ALL SALESMANS:

We ben spending two much time trying to spel instead of trying to sel. Lets watch thoes sails. I want everybody shud reed these leters frum Gooch, who is on the rode doin a grate job for us, and you shud go out and do like he done!

Never Try to Teach a Pig to Sing

86. What the Admiral Wanted

The process of revision can lead to great distortion. Depending upon how many links there are in the revision process, the distortion can run from slight to enormous. The following item from Oakland in 1987 purports to show how an original request can be altered by the different individuals or departments who were part of the production sequence. Although the text is ostensibly an account of U.S. Naval procedure, the use of NAVSEC instead of SECNAV, the standard abbreviation for the civilian Secretary of the Navy, suggests the item is popular in non-military sectors. The basic technique of the item is strongly reminiscent of "Project Swing" (cf. WH, 167).

AS OPNAV REQUESTED IT

AS NAVSHIPS APPROVED IT

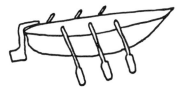

AS NAVSEC DESIGNED IT

AS THE CONTRACTOR MADE IT

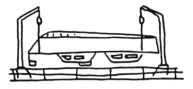

AS THE SHIPYARD INSTALLED IT

WHAT THE ADMIRAL WANTED

87. The Way You Ordered It

If too little organization is a vice, so also too much organization can lead to disaster. By the time an idea or order makes its way through the chain of command, it may well lose something in the transmission process. The following short series of cartoons was collected in Indianapolis in 1976.

The Way You Ordered It

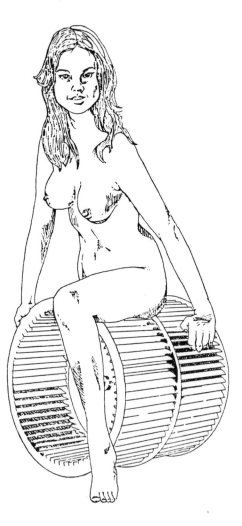

The Way We Designed It

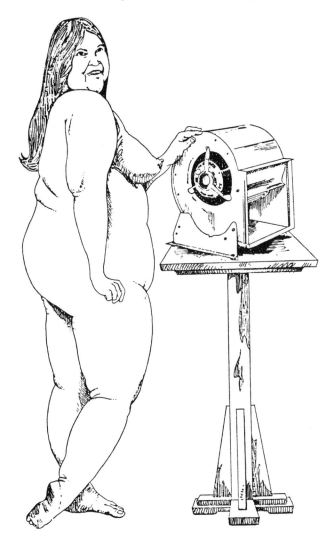

The Way Manufacturing Built It

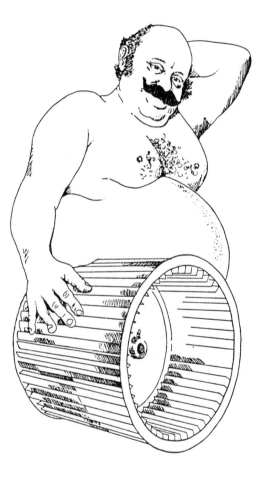

The Way We Shipped It

88. The Plan

For those who tend to make business a religion, it is easy to understand why a company plan might be couched in pseudo-biblical language. The initial portion of the following item collected in Orlando, Florida, in 1987, is surely a conscious echo of Genesis in the Old Testament. The final authority who approves the proposal—in some versions it is the commanding officer or the chairman of the board—is analogous to God.

The curious fact that the impetus for the plan is a crock of shit supports the notion that male creation myths may have an anal-erotic basis, e.g., the creation of the world from mud or the creation of man from dust. (One of the other versions is entitled "The Creation.") For an English version, see RIF, 109.

THE PLAN

In the beginning was the PLAN, and then the ASSUMPTIONS:
And the PLAN was without form, and the ASSUMPTIONS
    were VOID:
And darkness was upon the faces of the IMPLEMENTORS:

And they went to their Manager
    and spake unto him, saying:
  "It is a crock of shit,
    and it stinketh."

And the Manager went to the 2nd Level Manager
    and spake unto him, saying:
  "It is a crock of excrement,
    and none may abide the odor thereof."

And the 2nd Level Manager went to the 3rd Level Manager
    and spake unto him, saying:
  "It is a container of excrement,
    and it is very strong, such that none may abide before it."

And the 3rd Level Manager went to the Headquarters
Director
    and spake unto him, saying:
  "It is a vessel of fertilizer,
    and none may abide its strength."

And the Director went to the Division Vice President
and spake unto him, saying:
"It contains that which aids plant growth,
and it hath great strength."

And the Vice President went to the Division President
and spake unto him, saying:
"It promoteth growth,
and it is very powerful."

And the Division President went before the Board of
Directors
and spake unto them, saying:

"THIS POWERFUL NEW PLAN WILL PROMOTE
THE GROWTH OF THE COMPANY!"

. . . and, seeing that it was righteous and good,
the Board approved the PLAN.

89. Problem Solving Flowsheet

The computer has revolutionized thinking about problem solving. The computer's programming is based upon a binary system. This method of binary alternatives is the subject of the following text collected in Torrance, California, in 1988. This item is very widespread and popular. Alternative titles include: "Logical Troubleshooting," "Troubleshooting Procedure," "Troubleshooting Flowchart," and "Diagnostic Flow Chart," among others. It should be noted that all alternative paths do manage to end with "No Problem."

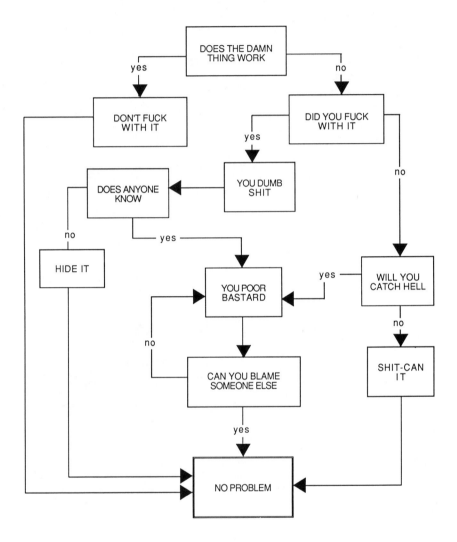

PROBLEM SOLVING
FLOWSHEET

Never Try to Teach a Pig to Sing

90. Warning!

As the modern office worker has come to depend more and more upon machines—electric typewriters, photocopy machines, telecopier machines, personal computers, and associated work stations, etc.—he or she has also had to learn how to cope with mechanical failures. The ability of machines to perform essential services is truly revolutionary, but by the same token, a prolonged machine breakdown can seriously impair office efficiency. Not surprisingly there is a marked tendency to anthropomorphize office machines and to endow them with human personality traits. As one may love one's machine when it performs well, so one may hate the same machine when it malfunctions. The following item from Raleigh, North Carolina, in 1988, pretends to offer advice on what to do during a machine breakdown. Particular attention is paid to the emotional state of the machine user. For another version, see YD [35].

WARNING !

This machine is subject to breakdowns during periods of critical need.

A special circuit in the machine called a 'critical detector' senses the operator's emotional state in terms of how desperate he or she is to use the machine. The 'critical detector' then creates a malfunction proportional to the desperation of the operator. Threatening the machine with violence only aggravates the situation. Likewise, attempts to use another machine may cause it to also malfunction. Keep cool and say nice things to the machine. Nothing else seems to work.

*Never let anything mechanical
know you are in a hurry*

91. To Err Is Human

In theory, computers are remarkable examples of modern technology designed to facilitate and expedite a variety of tedious tasks. However, in practice, computers turn out to be subject to the frailties of their human programmers. The following item collected from an Oakland urologist's office in 1989 takes its point of departure from a classic line of poetry penned by Alexander Pope in his 1711 "An Essay on Criticism." The line (from Part II, line 325) in full is: "To err is human, to forgive divine." This single line from the essay has apparently entered oral tradition. A Wellerism parody goes as follows: "'To err is human,' said the rooster as he climbed off the duck." In the item below, which was obtained originally by the urologist's nurse from a computer supply company in Scotts Valley, California, the reference to a computer substitutes in the slot initially occupied by the divine.

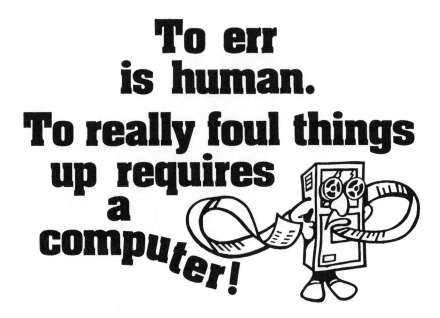

92. I Want My Data Back

Strange as it might appear at first glance, there are documented cases of outraged individuals taking out their frustration by hitting a machine, e.g., a soft-drink vending machine which failed to dispense a drink or return one's money. In the case of computers, there is a large number of reports of data mysteriously being erased or rendered momentarily irretrievable. The frustration level in such instances is high. The following text from Walnut Creek, California, in 1989, graphically illustrates that kind of emotion. The use of a handgun to resolve an emotionally trying situation may constitute a folk commentary on the widespread use of firearms in all kinds of urban disputes.

Never Try to Teach a Pig to Sing

93. Hit Any Key to Continue

The following item, collected from a trucking company in Eureka, California, in November 1989, also displays imminent violence toward a machine. In this case, a thoroughly discouraged duck stands on tiptoe to follow the computer-generated directions as to how to proceed. The tears of the thwarted duck may represent exasperation or anger or sadness or a combination of these emotions. Through animistic thought, the machine is endowed with anthropomorphic characteristics and thus becomes an appropriate object of physical punishment.

"HIT ANY KEY TO CONTINUE"

94. You'll Never Get It In

Another common source of frustration in urban America is parking. The fruitless search for a parking space in over-crowded cities can be an exercise in futility. In those cases where someone has parked poorly and occupied parts of two separate spaces (thereby eliminating at least one otherwise available space), the driver in search of a haven may express righteous indignation by leaving a message of the kind found on the wallet card presented here. Collected in San Francisco in 1983, it makes a direct analogy between parking and sexual intercourse.

95. Operation to Make Me Sterile

The proliferation of birth control techniques in the modern world has not yet solved the problems of unwanted pregnancies. In the following text from Manchester, England, in 1978, a simpleton seeks professional help. Because of his and his wife's inability to understand the mechanics of diverse methods of contraception, he is forced to take a desperate measure. For another English text, see TCB, 126.

Dear Sir,

I wish to apply for an operation to make me sterile. My reasons are numerous and after being married for seven years and having seven children, I have come to the conclusion that contraceptives are totally useless.

After getting married, I was told to use the Rhythm method. Despite trying the Tango and Samba my wife fell pregnant and I ruptured myself doing the Cha Cha Cha apart from which where do you get a band at five o'clock in the morning.

A doctor suggested we use the 'Safe Period'. At that time we were living with the in laws and we had to wait three weeks for a safe period when the house was empty. Needless to say this didn't work.

A lady of several years experience informed us that if we make love whilst breast-feeding we would be alright. It's hardly Newcastle Brown Ale, but I did finish up with clear skin, silky hair and wife pregnant.

Another old wives' tale was if my wife jumped up and down after intercourse this would prevent pregnancy. After constant breast feeding from my earlier attempt if my wife jumped up and down she would finish up with two black eyes and eventually knock herself unconscious.

I asked a chemist about the 'Sheath'. The chemist demonstrated how easy it was to use, so I bought a packet. My wife fell pregnant again which doesn't suprise me as I fail to see how Durex stretched over the thumb as the chemist showed me, can prevent babies.

She was then supplied with the coil and after several unsuccessful attempts to fit it, we realised we had got a left hand thread and my wife is definitely a right hand screw.

The 'Dutch Cap' came next. We were very hopeful of this as it did not interfere with our sex life at all. But alas it did give my wife severe headaches. We were given the largest size available but it was still too tight across her forehead.

Finally we tried the 'Pill'. At first it kept falling out. Then we realised we were doing it wrong. My wife then started putting it between her knees, thus preventing me from getting anywhere near her. This did work for a while until the night she forgot the pill. You must appreciate my problem. If this operation is unsuccessful, I will have to revert to oral sex, although, just talking about it can never be a substitute for the real thing.

Yours sincerely,

Dick Sinagen

Never Try to Teach a Pig to Sing

96. Turn Upside Down

A literal understanding or misunderstanding of an instruction is a popular device in folklore. Typically it is a metaphor which is wrongly interpreted literally, but in the present instance, it is a literal instruction which is misread. The following item was collected from New Baltimore, Michigan, circa 1981. In an English text, also involving a fire extinguisher, the caption or sign reads: "In Case of Fire, Gather up as much paperwork as possible and run towards the flames." See YWIW [118].

97. Polish Canoe Builder

Another traditional illustration of miscalculation takes the form of a canoe whose ends don't match. In some versions, the canoe is called an Italian rather than a Polish canoe. In others, there is no ethnic designation. This again suggests that it is the human condition which is primary, not the ethnic slur. In a day of increased technical specialization, an individual who attempts a "do-it-yourself" project frequently courts disaster. This text was collected in Indianapolis in 1976. The second text, a different cartoon, has a similar caption. Collected from Honeywell in Silverdale, Washington, in 1978, it also suggests a failure in construction. In this instance, improper bolting allows a seaplane's pontoons to become detached during take-off. For English versions, see OHB, 34; YWIW [31]; RIF, 80. For a Swedish version, see MF, 67.

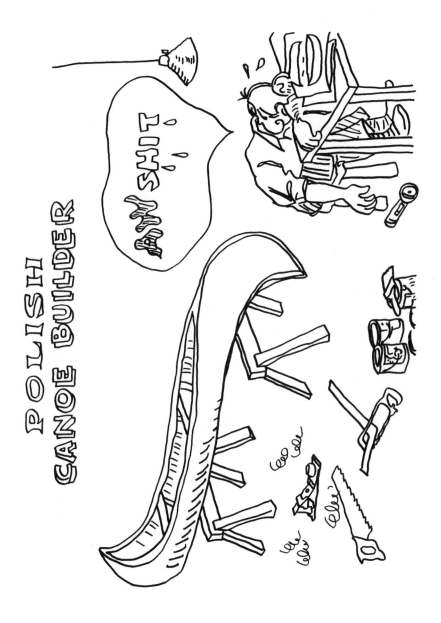

Never Try to Teach a Pig to Sing

98. On Recent Trip to U.S.

The Japanese are interested observers of American culture, many parts of which surely remain obscure to them (just as much of Japanese culture is not well understood by Americans). In the following text from Detroit in 1983, a Japanese gentleman is depicted as being confused about the game of golf (which has become increasingly popular in Japan). The fact that the item was collected in Detroit, the heart of the American automobile industry, tempts us to speculate about the resentment of that industry of the great Japanese success in exporting their many cars to the United States and the possible connection between that resentment and the impulse to make fun of a Japanese individual wearing an A-OK button.

ON RECENT TRIP
TO U.S. OBSERVED
HONORABLE AMERICANS
ON PLACE CALLED GOLF COURSE
PLAYING GAME CALLED
"AH SHIT!"

Never Try to Teach a Pig to Sing

99. Bulletin

In some busy shops, patrons are asked upon entering to take a number which is intended to guarantee service in an orderly and fair manner generally conforming to the adage "First come, first served." This practice is involved in the following item collected in Santa Clara, California, in 1989. The item also parodies overly intrusive governmental regulations with respect to industrial safety. In American folk speech, to "ride" someone implies a nagging, harassing action.

BULLETIN

The Occupational Safety and Health Administration (OSHA) has determined that the maximum safe load capacity on my butt is two persons at one time, unless I install handrails or safety straps. As you have arrived sixth in line to ride my ass today, please take a number and wait your turn.

Thank you.

100. Please Take a Number

Before one takes a number in a shop, one might pause to assess how much time it will take before being waited upon. This can be done by reading an electric sign indicating the number presently being attended to or by listening to a salesperson calling out the number of the next customer. By comparing that number with the number about to be taken (often in the form of a paper ticket or plastic card), a person can gauge the approximate waiting time for service.

The following item parodies the waiting time in a store with a cobweb suggesting how slow the service is, not to mention the numerical disparity between the customers at the front and the end of the line. The presence of the smiling face, virtually ubiquitous in the United States, belies the aggravation and frustration inherent in the long wait required. The item was collected from New Baltimore, Michigan, in 1981.

101. Keep Smiling

Americans delight in optimistic slogans such as "Have a Nice Day" and "Keep Smiling" which they persist in using regardless of the appropriateness of the social situation. The following item, found in the Supply and Maintenance office of the Main Library on the University of California, Berkeley, campus, contrasts the plight of an individual with the stereotyped, saccharine counsel. The forced smile of the victim underscores the inanity of the caption.

KEEP SMILING!

102. Even When You're Down and Out

In contrast to the "Keep Smiling" philosophy, there is the darker view of the grim realist. According to the latter perspective, it's a dog-eat-dog world and one expects weakness to be taken advantage of. Whether it is being victimized by the pecking order in an organizational hierarchy or being humiliated by a crowd of former colleagues, it is not always easy to keep smiling under such circumstances. In a true rat race, someone has to lose (compare with item 29). The first version came from Berkeley in 1988 while the second was collected in Dallas, Texas, in 1989. The third version was found in a General Electric plant in San Jose, California, in 1988.

EVEN WHEN YOU'RE DOWN AND OUT.
EVERYONE WANTS TO SCREW YOU !

Never Try to Teach a Pig to Sing

MY
BUDDIES!

Never Try to Teach a Pig to Sing

103. How My Day Went

Another common cliché is "How was your day?" or "How did your day go?" It may be asked by a friend or spouse at the end of a workday. Normally the response is equally trite: "Nothing special" or "It was great, how was yours?" But on a day when things went wrong, one might not be so willing to respond to a cliché in kind. In the following cartoon collected from an IBM office in the Bay Area circa 1980, the rat race is clearly over for the individual depicted. On the other hand, despite the plight of the poor victim, he is evidently still mobile, bouncing along on his tail or rear end.

HOW IN THE HELL DO YOU THINK MY DAY WENT ?

From Bad to Verse

Folk poetry is probably best known in its oral form. Yet there is a substantial number of folk poems which have been transmitted for decades in written form — first as hand-copied texts, later through typewritten copies and through ditto and mimeograph, and finally via photocopy machine. Some specimens of such folk poetry emphasize sentimental and nostalgic themes such as friendship or longing for the good old days of times past. Others contain ribald content.

Folk poetry, in contrast to the other genres transmitted by the office copier, is often claimed to have been composed by various individuals or is commonly attributed to specific authors although such attributions are often demonstrably false. Presumably there is always an individual poet who first composes folk poems, but in the vast majority of cases, the poet's name is not passed on. Typically, the sheet of paper upon which the poem is found has "author unknown" or "anonymous" following the poem's last line.

While elitist literary critics may disdain folk poetry of the kind presented here, the fact remains that these poems must have touched the responsive chords of a large number of individuals for them to have been passed on from generation to generation. These folk poems, then, may be said to have passed the test of time, surely a valid test of a poem's ultimate artistic worth.

One would not expect to find many close analogs of American folk poems transmitted by photocopier in non-English-speaking countries. Poems are fixed-phrase and cannot be easily translated from one language to another. (When one attempts to translate a poem from one language into another, one winds up writing a new poem!) Published collections of photocopier folklore from other countries do not include folk poetry as a rule. We suspect that each country may well have its own repertoire of folk poetry passed on by the photocopier, but this will have to be confirmed by future collections.

104. The Man in the Glass

One has obligations to family and to friends, but in the final analysis, one has to face himself with respect to judging how well or how poorly one has lived. This is the basic theme of a folk poem entitled "The Man in the Glass." When this poem was published in an Ann Landers newspaper column in 1983, it precipitated a rash of letters claiming authorship of the poem. Ann Landers presented selected excerpts from sample letters. They included the following. From a woman in Lafayette, Indiana: "My father wrote that poem in 1943, when I was in high school." An informant from Dayton, Ohio, said, "My aunt wrote it when she taught school in Alexandria, Louisiana." A man from Wellington, Kansas, wrote indignantly, "How dare someone take credit for my poem . . . I wrote it when I was a junior at Kansas University." A woman from New York suggested the poem "was probably composed by someone in the public relations department of Avon Products." The director of an alcoholism treatment center in Massachusetts declared angrily, "What blatant plagiarism! 'The Man in the Glass' was written by a patient here in 1967." An individual from Honolulu was equally offended. He maintained that the poem "was written by me in 1970 when I was recovering from alcoholism. I should have had it copyrighted. People have been stealing it left and right." A man from Chicago stated, "the author is Dale Wimbrow," while a reader from Arlington Heights, Illinois, stated, "the author was a member of A.A. who came from Pueblo, Colorado." Finally, a New Yorker contended that the poem "was translated from Italian and is well known in Catholic circles as 'The Prayer of Serenity.'" For these and other quotes, see Ann Landers, "Looking for the 'Man in the Glass,'" *Contra Costa Times*, Monday, December 5, 1983, p. 68.

While it is perfectly possible that one of the above mentioned writers is in fact the actual author of the poem, it is obviously not possible for *all* of them to have written the poem. One suspects that none of the above wrote the poem. Folklore is in the public domain and so anyone can and often does claim authorship of items of folklore. In any event, this poem continues to circulate as an anonymous creation. The version presented here was collected in Indianapolis in 1976.

THE MAN IN THE GLASS

When you get what you want in your struggle for
    self
And the world makes you king for a day,
Just go to a mirror and look at yourself
And see what THAT man has to say.

For it isn't your father or mother or wife
Whose judgement upon you must pass;
The Fellow whose verdict counts most in your
    life
Is the one staring back from the glass

You may be like Jack Horner and chisel a plum
And think you're a wonderful guy,
But the man in the glass says you're only a bum
If you can't look him straight in the eye.

He's the fellow to please, never mind all the rest
For he's with you clear up to the end,
And you've passed your most dangerous, difficult
    test
If the man in the glass is your friend.

You may fool the whole world down the pathway
    of years
And get pats on the back as you pass
But your final reward will be heartaches and
    tears
If you've cheated the man in the glass.

                  —Anonymous

105. Here and There

No matter how important an individual is, or thinks he is, the system can survive without him. Business, like life itself, must go on in spite of the loss of individuals. This humbling thought is the subject of the following folk poem collected in Washington, D.C., in 1976. The phrase "There is no indispensable man" is attributed to President Franklin Delano Roosevelt in a campaign speech he made in New York City in November, 1932. Whether the phrase stimulated the poem or whether Roosevelt took the phrase from an already existing folk poem is unclear. For English versions, see YWIW [22] and RIF, 105.

HERE AND THERE

Sometime, when you're feeling important,
Sometime, when your ego's in bloom,
Sometime, when you take it for granted
You're the best qualified in the room
Sometime when you feel that your going
Would leave an unfillable hole,
Just follow this simple instruction
And see how it humbles your soul:
Take a bucket and fill it with water,
Put your hand in it, up to the wrist,
Pull it out, and the hole that's remaining,
Is a measure of how you'll be missed.
You can splash all you please when you enter,
You can stir up the water galore,
But stop, and you'll find in a minute,
That it looks quite the same as before.
The moral in this quaint example,
Is to do just the best that you can.
Be proud of yourself, but remember,
There is no indispensable man!

106. Around the Corner

A sad and nostalgic folk poem presents quite another view of the passage of life. This version was collected from an office in Kokomo, Indiana, in 1967.

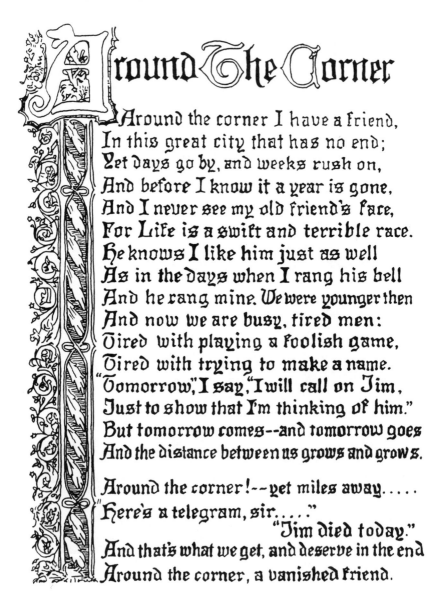

Around the corner I have a friend,
In this great city that has no end;
Yet days go by, and weeks rush on,
And before I know it a year is gone,
And I never see my old friend's face,
For Life is a swift and terrible race.
He knows I like him just as well
As in the days when I rang his bell
And he rang mine. We were younger then
And now we are busy, tired men:
Tired with playing a foolish game,
Tired with trying to make a name.
"Tomorrow," I say, "I will call on Jim,
Just to show that I'm thinking of him."
But tomorrow comes--and tomorrow goes
And the distance between us grows and grows.

Around the corner!--yet miles away.....
"Here's a telegram, sir....."
                    "Jim died today."
And that's what we get, and deserve in the end
Around the corner, a vanished friend.

107. A Crazy Recitation

A stylistic feature found in folk poetry is that of oxymoronic construction. One of the best-known examples is "The sun so hot I froze to death" in the Stephen Foster song "Oh Susanna." Another classic instance is the favorite children's poem which begins: "One bright day in the middle of the night, / Two dead boys got up to fight." The folk poem "A Crazy Recitation" belongs to the same genre. As the title itself suggests, the poem was popular in oral tradition. However, some informants chose to write it down and reproduce it by photocopier.

The first version was collected in Richmond, California, in 1969, from a seventy-one-year-old woman who claimed to have known it in her youth. The second version was collected in 1964 in San Rafael, California, from a woman who had learned it from her schoolmates in Chicago circa 1924.

The first two lines of the second stanza of our first version were reported from children in different parts of Britain by the Opies. See Iona and Peter Opie, *The Lore and Language of Schoolchildren* (London: Oxford University Press, 1959), p. 24; for a full text of "One bright day in the middle of the night," see p. 25. The final stanza of both versions also occurs separately as a folksong entitled "While the Organ Pealed Potatoes," sung to the tune of "Silver Threads among the Gold." For a text, see Marcia and Jon Pankake, *A Prairie Home Companion Folk Song Book* (New York: Viking, 1988), p. 190.

A Crazy Recitation

It was midnight on the ocean, not a streetcar was
    in sight,
The sun was shining brightly, and it rained all
    day that night.
It was evening and the rising sun was setting in
    the West.
The fishes in the pine trees were all cuddled in
    their nests.

'Twas a summer's day in winter, the snow was
    raining fast.
A barefoot girl with shoes on stood sitting on the
    grass.
The rain was pouring downward, the moon was
    shining bright,
And everything that you could see was hidden
    out of sight.

While the organ peeled potatoes, lard was
    rendered by the choir.
While the sexton rang the dishrag, someone set
    the church on fire.
"Holy smoke!" the parson shouted, and the poor
    guy lost his hair,
And now his head is just like heaven, for there is
    no parting there.

* * * * * * * *

O 'twas midnight on the ocean, not a streetcar
    was in sight
I went into a cigar store to ask the man for a
    light.
The man behind the counter was a woman old
    and gray
Who used to peddle doughnuts on the road
    to Mandalay.
Her children were all orphans, save one — a tiny
    tot
Who lived in the house across the street, right
    over the vacant lot.
"A very good evening, sir", he said and his eyes
    were dry with tears.
As he looked out of the open door he looked
    back over his ears.
The organ peeled potatoes, lard was rendered by
    the choir
While the sexton rang the church bells, someone
    set the church on fire.
"Holy smoke!" the minister shouted, in the
    rush he lost his hair
Now his head resembles heaven, 'cause there
    ain't no parting there.

108. A Little Mixed Up

While children may delight in intentional nonsequiturs, the older generation may perceive such phenomena in a different light. As more and more Ameicans live longer, there is increasing concern with some of the ailments that occur in old age. Failing memory is one such area of anxiety. The following folk poem collected in Patterson, New York, in 1987, illustrates some of the most common manifestations of poor memory.

A version collected in Walnut Creek, California, in 1989, contains an additional stanza which appears between the first two stanzas below:

> I got used to my arthritis,
> To my dentures I'm resigned,
> I can manage my bifocals,
> But God I miss my mind.

Still another version from Oakland in 1983 contains an additional final stanza:

> I stand beside my desk now
> And my head is bowed in shame.
> I'd readdress this letter.
> But I just forgot—your name.

It is interesting that there is an oral joke which parallels in part the content of the folk poem. The joke goes as follows. Three old women are sitting around a table talking. One complains, "My memory isn't what it used to be. I often find myself at the mailbox, and I can't remember if I am mailing a letter or picking up the mail. Sometimes I find myself back in the house with a letter I meant to post." A second woman is sympathetic. "I have the same problem. I often find myself at the refrigerator, and I can't remember if I'm there to put something in it or to take something out. Sometimes I walk away with a dish that I meant to store in the refrigerator." The third woman says emphatically, "Well, I don't have that problem. There's nothing wrong with my memory" and so saying, she raps three times on the table—to knock on wood (as a typical apotropaic gesture). A second or two later, the same third woman turns toward the door, saying, "Come in!"

"A LITTLE MIXED UP"

Just a line to say I'm living,
That I'm not among the dead;
Though I'm getting more forgetful,
And more mixed up in the head.

For sometimes, I can't remember,
When I stand at the foot of stairs,
If I must go up for something,
Or I've just come down from there.

And before the frig' so often,
My poor mind is filled with doubt,
Have I just put food away or
Have I come to take some out?

And there's times when it is dark out,
With my night cap on my head,
I don't know if I'm retiring,
Or just getting out of bed?

So, if it's my turn to write you,
There's no need in getting sore,
I may think that I have written,
And don't want to be a bore.

So, remember—"I DO LOVE YOU",
And I wish that you were here;
But now, it's nearly mail time,
So I must say "Good-bye, dear".

There I stood beside the mailbox,
With a face so very red,
Instead of mailing you my letter,
I opened it instead.

109. Old Age Is Hell

Old age may involve far more than failing memory. Other parts of the body may begin to show signs of wear and tear. Although one sometimes hears reference to retirement age as the "golden years," physical infirmities may tarnish reality. In the following item collected from Walnut Creek, California, in 1989, we find a negative paen to old age. The elaborate artwork, evidently computer generated, shows various dinosaurs, presumably equating old age with extinction. The image at the top center is meant to evoke the celebrated "American Gothic" painting by Grant Wood which shows an elderly farm couple standing solemnly and grimly in front of their homestead.

OLD AGE IS HELL

The body gets stiff, you get cramps in your legs
    Corns on your feet as big as hen eggs.
Gas in your stomach, elimination is poor.
    Take Ex-Lax at night, and then you're not sure.
You soak in the tub or your body will swell.
It's just like I said, "<u>OLD AGE IS HELL</u>."

The teeth start decaying, eyesight is poor
    Hair falling out all over the floor.
Sex life is shot, it's a thing of the past
    Don't kid yourself, friend, even that doesn't last.
Can't go to parties, don't dance any more.
    Just putting it mildly- you're a hell of a <u>bore</u>.

Liquor is out, can't take a chance.
    Bladder is weak, might pee in your pants.
Nothing to plan for, nothing to expect
    Just the mailman with your security check.

110. Yes Progress, That's Our Motto

This piece of folk poetry pokes fun at progress. Some basic activities and attitudes remain constant across the ages. For those individuals who find it wearing to keep pace with the rapidly accelerating technological changes in the modern world, the following poem collected in Bloomington, Indiana, in 1961, but surely going back to the turn of the century, may prove most welcome. The second version, collected in Indianapolis in 1976, bore the notation "Anon—circa 1909."

While it would be folly to oppose all progress in the technological sphere, it is equally foolish to accept blindly all the newfangled gadgets and gimmicks cranked out by the scientific-industrial complex. Artificial sweetners, preservatives, aerosol sprays, pesticides, drugs such as Thalidomide (which caused severe birth defects), the use of asbestos, etc., sometimes turn out to have unexpected side effects and grave if not lethal consequences. In the poem, the references to horseless carriages and seedless fruits may date it somewhat, but the sentiments expressed remain timely.

STRANGE ELECTRICAL APPLIANCES
HAVE SUPERSEDED STEAM
AND THE OLD TIME SAILING VESSEL
IS AN ANTIQUATED DREAM
WE HAVE OUR HORSELESS CARRIAGES
THAT ARE DRIVEN BY THE RICH
AND OUR WOMEN WEAR SILK HOSIERY
YET NEVER KNIT A STITCH
WE HAVE OUR SEEDLESS FRUITS
THAT NEVER SAW A BOUGH
EAT LOTS OF CREAMERY BUTTER
THAT NEVER SAW A COW
THE STOMACH ACHE WE USED TO HAVE
IS APPENDICITIS NOW
YES PROGRESS, THAT'S OUR MOTTO
MODERN TIMES HAVE COME TO STAY
BUT THANK GOD!
WE GET OUR CHILDREN IN THE SAME OLD
    FASHIONED WAY.

Strange electrical devices
   have superseded steam.
The old sailing vessel
   is an antiquated dream

We have the horseless carriage
   That is driven by the rich
And women wear silk hosiery
   Who never knit a stitch.

We have Curtiss
   And his Aeroplane
And tungsten lamps have come to stay

But—Thank God!
   We make our children
      In that good, old-fashioned way.

111. Kiss Me Baby I'm Vaccinated

We are presenting two versions of the following letter in order to document its traditionality. Again, like all folklore, the range of variation within a common frame is extraordinary. The first version was collected in Daly City, California, in 1968, from a seventh-grade girl who had left it in the desk of a boy she thought was "cute." The second version comes from Port Chicago, California, and dates from 1956. The final four lines of the second version also occur independently as a wallet card entitled "Definition of a Kiss." Other wallet card definitions of kisses include:

Definition of a Kiss

A Kiss is a noun because it is common and
   proper.
A Kiss is a verb because it shows action.
A Kiss in an adjective because it describes.
A Kiss is a conjunction because it connects two
   people.

For a longer version of this definition, see *More Over Sexteen* (New York: Grayson, 1953), p. 158.

Definition of a Kiss

A mouth full of nothing, that tastes like heaven,
and
sounds like a cow pulling its foot out of mud.

Loveable City
Kissable State
Pardon me honey
I forgot the date

City of Love
State of Kisses
19 hugs and 68 kisses

Dear Love,

I love you darling honest I do. I love you sweetheart please love me too. Please love me true. Of all the boys I've ever met you're the guy I can't forget. Your heart is like a pot of gold, hard to get and harder to hold.

Adam kissed Eve and Eve kissed another so why in the world can't we kiss each other. Kisses spread germs so as it was stated but you can kiss me baby, I'm vaccinated. So this is my letter to you my dear. I'd express myself better if you were here.

Never the less
but just the same.
Pardon me honey
I forgot my name . . .

City of Hope
State of Wishes
19 Hugs
62 Kisses

Ice Cream City
Lemonade State
Excuse me Honey
I forgot our Date

Dearest Darling
Wrote with a pen sealed a kiss,
If you love me you'll answer this.
Of all the boys I've ever met,
You're the one I can't forget.
I had a heart a heart so true,
But now it's gone from me to you.
Now you have two and I have none
So care for it as I have done.
My heart is like a lump of gold
Hard to get and hard to hold.
Our eyes have met our lips not yet,
But just you wait I'll get you yet.
Kissing is a proper noun
Standing up or sitting down.
Kissing spreads germs a Doctor once stated.
Kiss me baby I'm vaccinated.

With Love Forever,

112. Here's My Toast

An important part of the folklore of drinking includes the art of toasting the health of one's friends. Toasts are obviously an oral poetic form, but groups of them typed on sheets of paper do circulate courtesy of the office copier. The following set of toasts collected in Buffalo in 1977 is representative. It should be noted that each of the toasts has its own separate history. For a valuable discussion of toasts, see G. Legman, "Bawdy Monologues and Rhymed Recitations," *Southern Folklore Quarterly* 40 (1976), 111–23.

HERE'S MY TOAST

May you live as long as you want to
May you want to as long as you live
If I am asleep when you want to, wake me
If I am awake and don't want to, make me.

Here's to you, I am glad that I metcha
And now that I metcha, I am glad that I
    letcha
And now that I letcha, I betcha I letcha
    again.

You will always have friends,
Some friends will peter out
But I will always be your friend,
Peter in or peter out.

Here's to the drink that creates fire
Here's to the drink that creates desire
Not the kind that burns down shanties
But the kind that brings down panties.

Here's to the girl in the little red shoes
She drinks my liquor, she drinks my booze
She has no cherry, but that is no sin
She has the box that the cherry came in.

Here's to the girl dressed in black
She's dressed so fine, there's nothing to
    slack
She feels so fine and kisses so sweet
She makes things stand that have no feet.

Here's to an hour of sweet repose
Tummy to tummy and toes to toes
Then after an hour of sweet delight
It's fanny to fanny for the rest of the night.

Now that I am old and feeble
And my pilot light is out
What used to be my sex appeal
is now my water spout.

I used to be embarrassed to make the
    thing behave
For every single morning it would stand
    and watch me shave
But now I am getting old and it gives me
    the blues
To have the thing hang down and watch
    me tie my shoes.

God made little boys, made them out of
    string
He had a little left and made a little thing
God made little girls, made them out of
    lace
He ran a little short and left a little space.

THANK GOD!

It would be tempting to simply list all of the many toast texts
in circulation, but a full-fledged collection of toasts would require
a book-length work, especially if one studied the accompanying
gestures and analyzed the actual drinking behavior involved. We
shall therefore confine ourselves to several additional examples including parallels to some of the individual texts above.

A printed text collected in Bloomington, Indiana, in 1961, but
dated 1942, goes as follows:

> Here's to the girl in the yellow slicker
> She likes her gin and she likes her liquor
> She lost her cherry, but that's no sin
> For she still has the crate that the fruit came in.

Among twenty toasts in the Folklore-Epigrams file at ISR collected
at the University of Texas in Austin in 1962, we find:

> Here's to the girl in the yellow slicker, she'll smoke your weeds and
> drink your liquor. She's no virgin, but that's no sin, she's still got
> the crate that the fruit came in.

Another of the 1962 Texas toasts is:

> Here's to the girl dressed in red, she'll hug you and kiss you and
> squeeze you in bed. She has no cherry, but that's no sin, she's still
> got the box that it came in.

The variation in these toast texts is, of course, characteristic of any true folkloristic form. Consider the following variant of the seventh toast in our selection, a variant which was collected in Washington, D.C., in 1976:

> Here's to the moment of sweet repose,
> Belly to belly and nose to nose,
> After that moment of supreme delight . . .
> It's fanny to fanny the rest of the night.

For another version of this toast, see WY, 185. See also RJ, 98.

One of the most interesting of the photocopied toasts, at least metaphorically speaking, compares a woman to a fruited vine. From the 1962 group of University of Texas texts in ISR:

> Here's to the woman that wonderful vine, she blossoms each month, bears fruit every nine. The only thing this side of hell that can get juice out of nuts without cracking the shell.

Another version from ISR transforms the vine:

> Here's to a woman beautiful and divine
> Who blossoms each month and bears fruit every
>   nine
> She is the only chemist this side of hell
> Who can take juice out of nuts
> Without breaking the shell.

For those readers who may know only the more common toasts (for example, the following three from the University of Texas in 1962: "Up to the lips, over the gums, look out stomach, here it comes;" "Here's to my wife and sweetheart, may they never meet;" and "Here's to you, so sweet and good. God made you, I wish I could"), it may come as a surprise to know that a rich tradition of toasts continues to thrive in American folklore. In the present context, it is at least worth observing how this genre is represented in the repertoire of materials transmitted by xerographic means.

113. Friends May Come

The following piece of folk poetry, collected in Bakersfield, California, in 1969, also occurs orally, sometimes as a mock toast. (It was in fact included in the previous item.) Legman (RDJ, 624) cites a variant text which he says appeared on a novelty greeting card bought in Washington, D.C., in 1940. The poem plays on the common pun of peter as phallus.

A popular oral joke is based on the same pun. For a text, see *Over Sexteen* (New York: Elgart, 1951), p. 35. The joke's premise involves a college football player named Peters who was injured. The college paper proposed the headline: "Team Will Play without Peters." A dean caught it before press and ordered the editor to change it. Next morning, the revised headline reads: "Team Will Play with Peters Out."

> "Friends may come and
> Friends may go and
> Friends may peter out.
> But come what may
> I'll always be your friend
> Peter in or peter out."

114. Retirement

Among the previous toasts (item 112) are two verses of a piece of folk poetry which goes back more than fifty years and which provides a poignant vignette of the decline of sexual drives with the onset of old age. The stereotyped association of old age and impotence is a popular theme in folklore. Vance Randolph, indefatigable collector of folklore from the Ozarks, recorded several versions, one of which he noted in 1948 came from a woman who claimed to have learned it from her husband in Anderson, Missouri, about 1932. See "Vulgar Rhymes from the Ozarks" (manuscript in ISR), p. 127.

The first version below was collected in Oakland, California, in 1980. A second version, somewhat abbreviated, is nevertheless of interest because it is accompanied by a silhouette. It is in ISR and was collected in Washington, D.C., in 1947. Other titles of this extremely popular item include: "An Old Man's Dream," "My Life," "Lament of a Mature Man," "Too Old for the Draft," and "The First Hundred Years Are the Hardest." For three other versions of this item, see "The Passing of Peter" in UFFC-TB, 119–21; for an English version, see RIF, 110. For a short poetic version unaccompanied by a drawing, see Harold H. Hart, ed., *The Complete Immortalia* (New York: Bell Publishing Company, 1971), p. 400.

RETIREMENT

MY NOOKIE DAYS ARE OVER,
MY PILOT LIGHT IS OUT.
WHAT USED TO BE MY SEX APPEAL,
IS NOW MY WATER SPOUT.
TIME WAS WHEN OF ITS OWN ACCORD,
FROM MY TROUSERS IT WOULD SPRING.
BUT NOW I HAVE A FULL TIME JOB,
TO FIND THE BLASTED THING.
IT USED TO BE EMBARRASSING,
THE WAY IT WOULD BEHAVE.
FOR EVERY SINGLE MORNING,
IT WOULD STAND & WATCH ME SHAVE.
AS OLD AGE APPROACHES,
IT SURE GIVES ME THE BLUES,
TO SEE IT HANG ITS WITHERED HEAD
AND WATCH ME TIE MY SHOES.

Never Try to Teach a Pig to Sing

MY BALMY DAYS ARE OVER—
MY FIRE IS ALMOST OUT—
WHAT USED TO BE MY MAGIC WAND
IS NOW MY WATER SPOUT.

115. Time Marches On

The sexual ages of man are sometimes accompanied by cartoon animal figures. In the following item, it is evidently the position of the bull's tail which presumably serves as a measurable index of virility. The first two versions were collected in Oakland in 1974. The third version, obviously closely related to the second, is from ISR and is dated 1947. Only the first version is in verse. Note the variety in captions. Note also the apparent "watershed" distinction in the second version between forty years and fifty years. Up to forty years, the bulls face slightly toward the right (toward the future?) whereas the bulls for fifty and sixty years face slightly left (toward the past?). For a discussion of the critical nature of the number forty, see Stanley Brandes, *Forty: The Age and the Symbol* (Knoxville: University of Tennessee Press, 1985).

TIME MARCHES ON

AGE OF 20 RARIN' TO GO

AGE OF 40, WILLIN' BUT SLOW

AGE OF 50 NEVER KNOWS WHEN

AGE OF 70 NEVER AGAIN

How old are you?

BIRTHDAY GREETINGS
Hope You Are Not Getting Old

116. The Horse and Mule
Live Thirty Years

Another traditional comparison of the longevity of man with other animals is concerned with alcohol rather than sex. The figure of three-score years and ten as a measure of the optimum length of human life is of some antiquity. It is found in a Psalm (90:10) and it also occurs in A. E. Housman's *A Shropshire Lad*.

The title of this item varies. A version in ISR dating back to 1947 (from Washington, D.C.) bears the title "Rum-Soaked Men." A version from 1951 (Chicago) is entitled "Liquor Lengthens Life?" A version collected in Oakland in 1974 is labeled "Old But How True." (This last version ends with the couplet "And some of us, a mighty few, / Keep drinking 'til we're 92.") The version presented here was collected in Alameda, California, in 1970.

> The horse and mule live thirty years
> And nothing know of wines and beers;
> The goat and sheep at twenty die
> But never taste of Scotch or Rye.
> The cow drinks water by the ton
> And when eighteen is almost done;
> The dog at fifteen cashes in
> Without the aid of rum or gin.
> The cat in milk and water soaks
> And then in twelve short years it croaks;
> The modest, sober, bone-dry hen
> Lays eggs for nogs and dies at ten.
> The lower animals are cursed
> Because they lack a liquor thirst;
> Oh, not for them the lusty song
> And noisy revel all night long;
> Oh, not for them the merry quips
> That freely flow from wine-wet lips.
> From birth they play a tragic part
> And stop before they fairly start.
> All animals are strictly dry,
> They sinless live and swiftly die;
> But sinful, ginful, rum-soaked men
> Survive for three-score years and ten.

117. To My Critics

Life consists of work and play but what a person does with his life should be his own business. On the other hand, peer judgment is always an influencing factor in deciding whether to behave virtuously or sinfully. In this folk poem, the individual uses a conventional act of defiance to show his final contempt for his critics. We have presented two versions to show the extent of variation. The first version, from San Francisco, dates from the 1950s, while the second was collected in Chicago in 1983. For another version, see *Maledicta* 8 (1984–85), 199; for an English version, see OHB, 56.

> When I'm in a sober mood,
> I smoke, chew and think—
>
> When I'm in a jolly mood,
> I gamble, screw and drink—
>
> When all little moods are over,
> And from this world I pass—
>
> May they bury me face downward
> So the world can kiss my ass.

TO MY CRITICS

When I am in a sober mood -
I worry - work - and think.
When I am in a drunken mood -
I gamble - fight - and drink.
But when all my moods are over
And the world has come to pass
I hope they bury me upside down
So the world can kiss my ass.

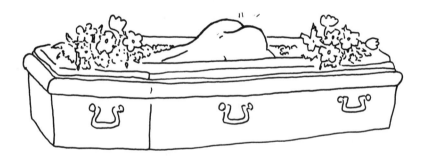

Never Try to Teach a Pig to Sing

118. Let's Be Friends

The common invitation which concludes the previous item is found in other contexts. The following item collected from the office of a brokerage firm in Carmel, California, in 1980, involves a double entendre political reference to the animal symbol of the Democratic Party, the donkey. The elephant, of course, is the equivalent totem for the Republican Party.

The phrase "kiss my ass" has parallels in other cultures. In Germany, for example, the analog is "lech mich im arsch" often abbreviated as LMIA. See Heinz-Eugen Schramm, *LMIA* (Gerlingen, 1967). For an extended discussion of the overall significance of the idiom in German culture, see Alan Dundes, *Life Is Life a Chicken-Coop Ladder: A Study of German National Character Through Folklore* (Detroit: Wayne State University Press, 1989), pp. 43–48. For a text which purports to explain why Democrats have more children than Republicans and ends with a reference to the unlikelihood of anyone enjoying a good piece of elephant, see *Playboy's Party Jokes 4* (Chicago: PBJ Books, 1970), p. 181.

GREETINGS FROM THE LOYAL OPPOSITION!

LETS BE FRIENDS

The election is over, the result is known
The will of the people is clearly shown
Lets forget our quarrels, and show by our deeds
We'll give our leader all the help he needs.
So lets all get together and let our bitterness pass
I'll hug your elephant, and you kiss my ass.

119. Thought for Today

Everyone knows the so-called Golden Rule: "Do unto others as you would have others [them] do unto you," or from Jesus' Sermon on the Mount as recorded in Matthew (7:12): "Therefore all things whatsoever ye would that men should do to you, do ye even so to them: for this is the law." The folk with their traditional healthy scepticism based upon years of experience with the pragmatics of daily life regard the rule with some suspicion. Novelist Edward Noyes Westcott (1846–98) in his 1898 book *David Harum* offered a pithy re-write: "Do unto the other feller the way he's like to do unto you an' do it fust [first]." The folk have a more vernacular rendering of the Golden Rule. In the following text from an Oakland real estate office in 1977, the very title "Thought for Today" sets up an expectation of a syrupy homily.

Thought for Today

"If you have a friend
  Who is kind and true,
Fuck him—before
  He fucks you"

120. When I Am Dead and in My Grave

Another pseudo-epitaph invites passersby to commemorate a full life. The epitaph genre typically involves a concern with death and religion. Epitaphs often express sentiment and review the achievements of the deceased. The following parody shows that nothing is too sacred for folk humor. Death and burial are made light of in this defiant invitation.

Of special interest is the explicit linkage between the final line and the longstanding Indo-European and Semitic notion that the dead are thirsty. The critical equation is: liquid = life. Thus the absence of liquid = death. This is why burial customs in India, Greece, and elsewhere commonly entail pouring water on the graves or gravestones of the deceased. See Giuseppe Bellucci, "Sul Bisogno di Dissetarsi Attribuito All'Anima dei Morti," *Archivio per l'Antropologia e la Etnologia 39* (1909), 211–99; and Waldemar Deonna, "Croyances funeraires: La soif des morts," *Revue de l'Histoire des Religions* 119 (1939), 53–81.

The version presented here is from ISR and was collected in Chicago in 1951. It is almost identical to a version circulating twenty-five years later in Kokomo, Indiana (not presented here). For other versions, see UFFC-TB, 122 and RIF, 101.

When I am dead and in my grave
No more pussy shall I crave
And on my tombstone shall be written
I've had my share and I ain't shittin'

* * * *

When I die, bury me deep
Make it simple, make it cheap
Upon my tombstone, I want this note
Millions of drinks went down my throat
And if you should pass by where I lie
Piss on me, I'm always dry.

121. Love

Some people drink because they feel unloved, but some people are unloved because they drink. Alcoholism is a serious problem and that is why there is so much folklore about drinking. The drunk is a standard character in many jokes and motion pictures.

The following short poem collected in Foster City, California, in 1986, answers the question of who could possibly love a drunk. For more examples of the folklore of alcoholism, see Ernest L. Abel, *Alcohol Wordlore and Folklore* (Buffalo: Prometheus Books, 1987).

LOVE

THE LOVE OF A BEAUTIFUL MAIDEN
THE LOVE OF A STATELY MAN
THE LOVE OF A BABY UNAFRAID
HAVE EXISTED SINCE TIME BEGAN

BUT THE GREATEST LOVE
   THE LOVE OF LOVES
EVEN GREATER THAN THAT OF A MOTHER

IS THE TENDER
   PASSIONATE
      INFINITE
         LOVE

OF ONE DRUNKEN SLOB FOR ANOTHER . . . .

122. I'm Fine

The state of one's health is an abiding concern for most individuals and their friends. Yet there is a problem in deciding how frank to be in discussing one's physical or mental condition. By far the leading American greeting formula upon meeting is "How are you?" It is not, however, normally regarded as a genuine request for information. Rather, politeness dictates that the reply consist of "[I'm] Fine, how are you?" This too is part of a verbal ritual exchange rather than truly indicating one's self-evaluation of one's health. Sometimes when a person is known to be in poor health or to have been ill, the introductory greeting formula addressed to that person might be: "How are you feeling?" But again the person in question is expected to answer: "I'm fine."

Details of illness are rarely welcome inasmuch as they serve to remind all of the participants in the conversation of their own mortality. The American ethos also prefers optimism to pessimism. Thus, rather than dwelling upon unpleasant or disagreeable facts, Americans are encouraged even as youngsters to look on the bright side. Yet the sad facts of illness and increasing physical debilitation with the passing years cannot be totally denied. The phrase in the following item "I'm awfully well for the shape I'm in" beautifully if somewhat sarcastically epitomizes the disparity between an individual's actual condition and the good face he is required to put on in public.

The following folk poem treats this convention of a person's insisting he is perfectly healthy in spite of a lengthy list of ailments. It was collected in Buffalo in 1977. (For a variant text, see UFFC-TB, 123.)

"I'm Fine"

"There's nothing whatever the matter with me
I'm just as healthy as I can be.
I have arthritis in both my knees,
And when I talk, I speak with a wheeze.
My pulse is weak and my blood is thin.
But, I'm awfully well for the shape I'm in.

I think my liver is out of whack,
And I have a terrible pain in my back.
My hearing is poor and my eyes are dim,
Most everything seems to be out of trim.

The way I stagger sure is a crime,
I'm likely to fall at any time.
But, all things considered I'm feeling fine.

Arch supports for both of my feet,
Or I wouldn't be able to walk down the street.
My fingers are ugly, stiff in the joints,
Complexion is bad, due to dry skin.
But, I'm awfully well for the shape I'm in.

My dentures are out, I'm restless at night,
In the morning I'm a frightful sight.
Memory's failing, head's in a spin,
I'm practically living on aspirin.
But, I'm awfully well for the shape I'm in.

Now the moral is, as this tale unfolds,
That for you and me who are growing old,
It's better to say, "I'm fine", with a grin,
Than to tell everyone of the shape we're in."

123. My Get Up and Go has Got Up and Went

Maintaining one's equanimity and sense of humor is tested in life not only by inevitable aches and pains but also by growing old. Old age is particularly difficult to face in American culture because Americans worship youth. Most societies of the world are past oriented and in theory, the older one becomes, the more respect one may acquire. In contrast, Americans are future oriented and senior citizens typically are objects of pity rather than respect. (For a further discussion of this tendency, see Alan Dundes, "Thinking Ahead: A Folkloristic Reflection of the Future Orientation in American Worldview," *Anthropological Quarterly* 42 [1969], 53–72.)

The following folk poem collected in San Francisco in 1976 but which circulated in the late 1950s reflects an admirably cheerful outlook toward advancing age. The narrator has become reconciled to the slower pace of the later years and with considerable flippant wit describes a daily routine. This version is untitled but other versions bear the title "My Get Up and Go Has Got Up and

Went." The poem also exists in oral tradition. In 1977, the authors saw a Sacramento woman being interviewed on television on the occasion of her one hundredth birthday. When asked by reporters how she felt, she answered by reciting several lines from this poem.

For a full text of this poem, see UFFC-TB, 124, where it is combined with item 122 in this volume. There is some evidence that these two items which do occur independently also exist in combination. For an English version, see TCB, 167.

How do I know my youth has been spent?
Because my get-up-and-go, got up and went.
But in spite of all that, I am able to grin
When I think where my get-up-and-go has been.

Old age is golden, I have heard it said,
But sometimes I wonder as I go to bed,
My ears in a drawer, my teeth in a cup,
My eyes on a table when I wake up.

Ere sleep dims my eyes I say to myself,
Is there anything else I should lay on the shelf?
But I am happy to say as I close the door
My friends are the same as in days of yore.

When I was young my slippers were red,
I could kick my heels right over my head,
When I grew older my slippers were blue,
But still I could dance the whole night through.

Now I am old, my slippers are black,
I walk to the corner and puff my way back.
The reason I know that my youth is spent
My get-up-and-go, got up and went.

But I really don't mind when I think with a
    grin
Of all the places my get-up has been,
Since I have retired from life's competition
I busy myself with complete repetition.

I get up each morning, dust off my wits,
Pick up the paper and read the obits,
If my name is missing I know I am not
    dead
So, I eat a good breakfast and go back to bed.

124. I Would Rather Be a Could Be

The sentiment in the previous poem is rather like another piece of folk poetry which takes pleasure in present living and in past achievement. According to this other short poem, having a happy and full life in the present is the ideal. Second best is a hopeful future. And third is having a past filled with achievement and satisfaction to look back on. This short poem was collected from oral tradition in Oakland in 1969 but it was said to have circulated in Kansas at the end of the nineteenth century.

> I WOULD RATHER BE A COULD-BE, IF I
> COULDN'T BE AN ARE.
> FOR A COULD-BE IS A MAYBE WITH A
> CHANCE OF TOUCHING PAR.
> I WOULD RATHER BE A HAS BEEN THAN A
> MIGHT-HAVE-BEEN BY FAR.
> FOR A MIGHT-HAVE-BEEN HAS NEVER
> BEEN, AND A HAS-BEEN WAS ONCE
> AN ARE.

125. The Bee Is Such a Busy Soul

The bee has fascinated humankind for centuries. The workings of the bee community, the construction of hives, and the production of honey have all contributed to the continuing interest in the life of the bee. No doubt the fear of a bee's sting has also played a part in the folk's conception of this insect. In any event, there are many similes and metaphors based upon the bee and its activities. "As busy as a bee" is certainly one of the most common folk similes in American folk speech. The bee's ability to reproduce has provided one half of the most widespread euphemism for human sexual activity: "the birds and the bees." Both these idioms are features in the following text from Sacramento in 1979, as well as a standard abbreviated form of the popular insult: son of a bitch.

The bee is such a
busy soul,
He has no time for
birth control.
And that is why
in times like these,
There are so many
sons of bees!

126. Ain't It the Truth

Sexual stereotypes insist upon differentiating male and female appetites. In the following item from ISR in the 1950s, the male's decreasing vigor is contrasted with the female's supposedly undiminished sexual capacity. In some versions of the last line of the first stanza, the reference is to "It's all in his mind" rather than "It's still in his mind" suggesting an even further if not complete deterioration of the male sexual drive.

The explicit male chauvinism of the second stanza reflects a lack of sensitivity characteristic of earlier eras and some would say today as well. The idea that a woman is "always inclined" is pure male fantasy and the suggestion that there is "nothing to get ready" demonstrates a total ignorance of women's sexual needs. The gratuitous remark implying that women are mindless sex objects is part of the same offensive stereotype.

Stereotypes die hard—if indeed they die at all. One reason for their persistence is the existence of folklore of this kind. For an English version, see TCB, 155.

AIN'T IT THE TRUTH

To Men

From 20 to 30 if a man lives right,
It's once in the morning and once in the night.
From 30 to 40 if he still lives right,
He cuts out the morning or else the night.
From 40 to 50 it's now and then,
From 50 to 60 it's God knows when.
From 60 to 70 if he is still so inclined
Don't let him kid you, for it's still in his mind.

To Women

With women it's different—it's morning and
     night,
Regardless whether they live wrong or right.
Age cuts no figure, they are always inclined,
Nothing to get ready, not even their mind.
So after all is said and done,
A man at 60 has completed his run.
The woman at 60—figures don't lie,
Can take the old root—till her time comes to die.
    I KNOW.

127. Woman!

Another male view of the female of the species is found in the following folk poem collected in Washington, D.C., in 1976. The poem consists of a series of binary oppositions purportedly describing the contradictory nature of women. For a version from Carlisle, Pennsylvania, dating from 1953–54, see Mac E. Barrick, "The Typescript Broadside," *Keystone Folklore Quarterly* 17 (1972), 28.

WOMAN!

Woman—She's an angel in truth, a demon in
    fiction.
A woman's the greatest of all contradictions;
She's afraid of a cockroach, she'll scream at a
    mouse.
She'll tackle a husband as big as a house.
She'll take him for better, she'll take him for
    worse,
She'll split his head open, and then be his nurse.
And when he is well and can get out of bed,
She'll pick up a tea pot and throw it at his head.
She's faithful, deceitful, keen sighted and blind;
She's crafty, she's simple, she's cruel, she's kind,
She'll lift a man up, she'll cast a man down,
She'll make him her hero, her ruler, her clown.
You fancy she's this, but you find that she's that,
She'll play like a kitten, and fight like a cat.
In the morning she will, in the evening she
    won't,
And you are always expecting she will, but she
    don't.

128. The Dogs Once Gave a Party

A dog is said to be man's best friend, and one aspect of that animal's behavior which has long intrigued human observers is its form of greeting. The greeting typically consists of one dog's sniffing the posterior of another.

The following folk poem represents a creative attempt to find an origin for this curious bit of dog etiquette. The text dates from about 1910 in San Francisco. We have taken the liberty of adding from other versions lines apparently omitted from this text. These added lines are contained in brackets. For other versions of this traditional poem, see "Why Dogs Leave a Nice Fat Bone" in *Immortalia* ([New York], 1927), p. 97, and "Sniff" in *Furthermore Over Sexteen*, Vol. 4 (New York: Grayson, 1956), p. 88.

The dogs once gave a party,
    They came from near and far;
Some came by auto,
    while others came by car.

But before they were allowed
    into the hall to take a look,
They had to take their ass-holes off,
    And hang them on a hook.

No more were they seated,
    [each mother, son and sire,]
than some dirty yellow cur
    Started in to holler, "Fire!"

[And out they rushed all in a bunch
    and had no time to look,]
And up they jumped at random,
    And grabbed an ass-hole off the hook,

They got the ass-holes all mixed up,
    Which made them very sore,
To have to wear an ass-hole
    That they never saw before.

And that's the reason why,
    As you go up and down the street,
Each dog you see will swap a smell
    with each dog he'd meet,

And that's the reason why a dog
    Will leave a nice fat bone,
To go and smell an ass-hole,
    For he hopes to find his own.

It is more than likely that this poem is based upon a folktale. The Grimm brothers, for example, collected a tale "Why Dogs Sniff One Another" some time before 1819 in Bavaria. In the Grimm tale, a dog at a feast is sent by the lion host to fetch some pepper, but the dog ran off with the pepper instead of returning to the banquet. Ever since, other dogs have sniffed one another to find the dog with the pepper. See Ruth Michaelis-Jena and Arthur Ratcliff, *Grimms' Other Tales* (London: Golden Cockerel Press, 1956), p. 140.

129. Pete the Piddling Pup

An unusual but certainly traditional parody of epic poetry concerns a legendary country canine hero named Pete (or in some versions Runt or Rex) who is challenged by his city confreres to a piddling match. The name Pete may or may not be related to the slang term "peter" meaning phallus. Alternate titles for this mock epic include: "Pete the Pedigreed Piddler" and simply "The Piddlin' Pup." While the quality of the verse is only fair—Legman somewhat uncharitably (but wittily) calls it doggerel (NLM, 896, cf. RDJ, 193)— the age-old struggles of country versus city, stranger versus ingroup, and individual versus gang (as in most American westerns) are all very much in evidence. Pete outshoots all his rivals and leaves town triumphant. The version presented here was collected in southern California in the late 1960s. For an earlier version entitled "The Diabetic Dog," see *Immortalia* ([New York], 1927), pp. 28–30.

PETE THE PIDDLING PUP

A farmer's dog once came to town,
His christian name was Pete
His pedigree was two miles long
And his looks were hard to beat
And as he trotted down the road
'Twas beautiful to see
His work on every corner
His work on every tree

He watered every gateway
He never missed a post
For piddling was his masterpiece
And piddling was his boast
The city dogs looked lovingly on
In deep and jealous rage
To see a simple country dog the piddler of his age.

Then all the dogs from far and wide
Were summoned with a yell
To sniff this country stranger off
And judge him by his smell
They sniffed beneath his stumpy tail
Their praise of him ran high
And when one sniffed him underneath
Pete piddled in his eye.

They smelled him over one by one
They smelled him two by two
And noble Pete in high disdain
Stood till they were through
Then Pete to show these city dogs
He didn't give a damn
Walked right into a grocer's shop
And piddled on a ham.

He piddled on the onions
He piddled on the floor
And when the grocer kicked him out
He piddled on the door
Behind him all the city dogs
Decided what they would do
They started a piddling carnival
To see the stranger through.

They'd show him all the piddling posts
They knew all round the town
They started off with many winks
To wear the stranger down
They called the champion piddlers
Who were always on the go
And sometimes held a piddling comp.,
Or had a piddling show.

They sprang this on him suddenly
When halfway through the town
But Pete just piddled on and on
And wore the champions down
For Pete was with them every trick
With vigour and with vim
A thousand piddles more or less
Were all the same to him.

From Bad to Verse

So he was kicking merrily
With hind legs kicking high
When most were lifting legs in bluff
And piddling mighty dry
On and on Pete sought new grounds
On which to lay the dust
Till every other dog went dry
And gave up in disgust.

But on and on went noble Pete
To water every sandhill
Till all the city champions
Were piddled to a standstill
Then Pete an exhibition gave
Of all the ways to piddle
Like "double trip" and "family flip"
And now and then a "dribble".

And all the time the country dog
Did neither wink nor grin
But piddled blithely out of town
As he had piddled in
The city dogs said "So long friend
Your piddling defeats us"
But no-one ever put them wise
That Pete had diabetes.

The length of the poem precludes detailing all the variations noted in different versions. We shall cite but one illustrative example. Compare the ninth stanza above with the equivalent stanza in a version from Alexandria, Virginia, collected in 1976:

But on and on went noble Runt
As wet as any rill
Till all the city champions
Were peed to a standstill.
Then Runt did free hand piddling
With fancy flips and flings
Like double dips and gimlet twists
And all those graceful things.

Different Strokes
for Different Folks

Folklore normally revolves around different groups. The groups may be defined by ethnicity, religion, race, occupation, geography, or other means. There is the folklore *of* groups and the folklore *about* groups. The folklore about groups often consists of stereotypes. Some stereotype folklore is cruel and hurtful, at least to the folk group being stereotyped. Yet it seems unlikely that the folklore of stereotypes will ever disappear. Whether it is management making fun of employees (or vice versa) or the young making fun of the old (or vice versa), the principle is the same. No group can feel superior except at some other group's expense. We can see this principle at work in the various traditional ethnic and racial stereotypes. (We shall reserve examples of sexist stereotypes for our final chapter.)

One difficulty in presenting the folklore of stereotypes is that the data may be considered offensive. Politicians have actually lost their jobs through the ill-advised telling of ethnic jokes. Media personnel, including disk jockeys and talk show hosts, have risked suspension or firing for the same reason. We want to make it clear that we present samples of folk stereotypes not to perpetuate them, but to illustrate their undeniable presence in office-copier tradition. Not to present them would be dishonest in our opinion. The materials exist—whether we report them or not. We believe that by identifying such materials as stereotypes, we may ultimately contribute to raising the levels of consciousness of those who pass on such materials and thus hopefully diminish the negative impact of these deplorable stereotypes.

130. Management/Employees

One of the characteristics of most organizations, including those in business, is social hierarchy. Most employees are junior to some individuals and perhaps at the same time senior to others. Typically, a senior takes out his or her aggression on a junior person. One familiar metaphor for expressing aggression is to "dump" on someone, meaning to defecate on the subordinate.

In the following cartoon collected in Berkeley in 1980, the double outhouse demonstrates the nature of this metaphor. In this case, management is higher up than the employees, and since they are directly over them, the employees cannot easily avoid being hit by unpleasant objects from above. It should be noted as well that one conventional sign of having moved successfully up the corporate ladder is the possession of a key (or access) to the executive bathroom. In that context, the choice of metaphor is certainly apt. (In another version from 1969—not presented here—the labeling is "Officers" and "Men," referring to military hierarchy.) For another version, see OHB, 1.

Different Strokes for Different Folks

131. Engineer/Salesman/Purchasing Agent

Stereotypes are not infrequently addressed to multiple groups simultaneously. Any joke beginning: "There was an Englishman, an Irishman, and a Scotsman" is almost certain to involve three distinct national stereotypes. Multiple-group slurs may be ethnic or they may be occupational, as in the following text from Foster City, California, in 1986.

Sometimes slurs are very specific with respect to alleged group characteristics, e.g., the supposed stinginess of Scotsmen, but in other instances, the slurs are virtually interchangeable. For example, the English consider the Irish to be stupid just as the French consider the Belgians to be and the Germans consider the East Frisians to be (and the Americans consider the Polish-Americans to be). The very same jokes are told about all of these "stupid" victim-groups. The stereotypes articulated in the occupational item below are *not* group-specific. Another version from San Leandro, California, in 1988 (not presented here), for example, speaks of an architect, engineer, and a contractor with a very similar text. For another version, see UFFC-TB, 110; for an English version, see TCB, 99.

In a second item from Hayward, California, collected in April 1990, we find quite a different stereotypic picture of engineers. They are perceived by rough and tough construction workers as being mincing, prancing effeminate creatures who sing formulas while holding hands. The cartoon also depicts the dichotomy between brawn and brains. The distinction is also manifested in differing dress codes. Hard hats, heavy work shoes, tools, and hairy arms and faces contrast with jaunty hats, pointy-toed shoes, bow ties, and quaint formal attire. The dance pose and the inane toothy grins of the effete engineers seem far removed from the earthy reality of the workaday world. There is also the implication that the engineers are prissy enough to be offended by construction-worker vernacular. In another version found in YD [148], two similar engineer figures are dressed in harlequin costumes, which surely connotes comic clown attributes. (For a completely different stereotype of the engineer as someone illiterate, see WY, 212–14; for a Swedish xerographic definition of an engineer, see MF, 52.)

Never Try to Teach a Pig to Sing

 **AN ENGINEER** is said to be a man who knows a great deal about very little and who goes along knowing more and more about less and less until finally he knows practically everything about nothing; whereas

A SALESMAN, on the otherhand, is a man who knows a very little about a great deal and keeps knowing less and less about more and more until he knows practically nothing about everything.

 **A PURCHASING AGENT** starts out knowing practically everything about everything, but ends up knowing nothing about anything, due to his association with engineers and salesman.

132. The Typical Auditor

The following item from Berkeley in 1980 pretends to describe the essential personality features of an auditor. Auditors are members of the accounting profession, and their responsibilities within an organization are frequently of a policing nature. They are charged with verifying inventories, expense accounts, purchases, payments, receipts, and the like. In another brief xerographic item, such an attitude is reflected in the statement: "Auditors are people who come in after the war is over and bayonet the wounded." Thus, they are often feared and disliked by other employees. A derogatory slang term for auditors is "bean counters," referring to their function of keeping track of miniscule quantities. Another slang term is "number crunchers," indicating the auditor's concern with numbers in financial projections or in profit and loss statements. For an English version, see TCB, 98.

" THE TYPICAL AUDITOR IS A MAN PAST MIDDLE AGE, SPARE, WRINKLED, INTELLIGENT, COLD, PASSIVE, NON-COMMITTAL, WITH EYES LIKE A CODFISH, POLITE IN CONTACT, BUT AT THE SAME TIME UNRESPONSIVE, COLD, CALM AND DAMNABLY COMPOSED AS A CONCRETE POST OR A PLASTER-OF-PARIS CAST; A HUMAN PETRIFICATION WITH A HEART OF FELDSPAR AND WITHOUT CHARM OF THE FRIENDLY GERM, MINUS BOWELS, PASSION, OR A SENSE OF HUMOR. HAPPILY THEY NEVER REPRODUCE AND ALL OF THEM FINALLY GO TO *HELL*. "

HERE HE STANDS

133. Heaven Is . . .

One of the classic multi-group national slurs has to do with a definition of the personnel to be found in heaven and hell. Heaven's staff invariably refers to positive stereotypes while hell's groups demonstrate strictly negative characteristics. The following text was collected from a U.S. Army dependents' school in Aschaffenburg, West Germany, in 1988. Another version was cited in *Parade Magazine* for January 1, 1989, p. 6:

> Heaven is an American salary, a Chinese cook, an English house and a Japanese wife. Hell is defined as having a Chinese salary, an English cook, a Japanese house and an American wife.

For other versions, see Alan Dundes, *Cracking Jokes* (Berkeley: Ten Speed Press, 1987), p. 106. See also YD [7]. For a German version, see IK, 32; for a Swedish version, see MF, 63.

Heaven is where the police are British, the cooks French, the mechanics German, the lovers Italian and it is all organised by the Swiss. Hell is where the chefs are British, the mechanics French, the lovers Swiss, the police German, and it is all organised by the Italians.

Never Try to Teach a Pig to Sing

134. Still Awaiting Instructions

The following text from Ontario, California, in 1989, is a localized version of a standard and widespread multi-group national slur. The informant in this instance was an employee of Kaiser Industries, formerly of Oakland, California. In one of a number of oral parallels, it is the Russians who are awaiting further instructions from Moscow. See Alan Dundes, *Cracking Jokes* (Berkeley: Ten Speed Press, 1987), p. 89.

BULLETIN

An Ocean Liner recently sank somewhere in the South Pacific leaving only 12 survivors who were fortunate enough to swim to a nearby island.
There were two French businessmen and their secretary
Two Italian businessmen and their secretary
Two British businessmen and their secretary
and two Kaiser executives and their secretary.

As of our last report, the two Frenchmen have worked out a compromise of one having the secretary on Monday, Wednesday and Friday, and the other on alternate days.

One Italian shot the other so he could have the secretary every day of the week.

The two British gentlemen shot their secretary so they could have each other.

The two Kaiser executives are still awaiting instructions from Oakland.

135. Children!

America is known for being a child-oriented culture, but that doesn't prevent parents from being annoyed if not harassed by know-it-all children. The first version of the following item was collected from a realtor's office in Cincinnati in 1988; the second from a doctor's office in Eureka, California, also in 1988.

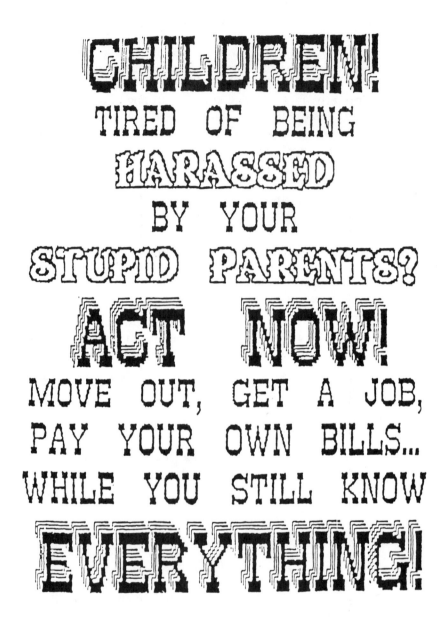

CHILDREN! TIRED OF BEING HARASSED BY YOUR STUPID PARENTS? ACT NOW! MOVE OUT, GET A JOB, PAY YOUR OWN BILLS... WHILE YOU STILL KNOW EVERYTHING!

TEENAGERS
Tired of being
HASSLED
by
UNREASONABLE PARENTS?
Then NOW is the
TIME FOR ACTION!!
Leave home and pay your own
way while you STILL
KNOW EVERYTHING !

136. Thank God for Medicare

The following joke tells how to take full advantage of Medicare. One of the common complaints about Medicare and other forms of socialized medicine is that it takes business away from private practice and places it in the public sector. In this case, a most private sexual relationship is exposed to an onlooker for purely financial reasons. The joke as it presently circulates in xerographic transmission could only have arisen after the advent of Medicare and sexual counseling clinics. The text presented here was collected in Concord, New Hampshire, in 1977. For an English version, see RIF, 113.

An elderly couple entered the doctor's office and were escorted by the nurse to the treatment room. When the doctor entered the room and asked what their problem was the old man said "we want you to watch us have sex relations to see if we are doing it right". The doctor agreed and later after they were dressed he gave his assurance that their sex performance was all right and charged them $10.00.

During the next month the same couple came back every four or five days and always with the same request. Curiosity finally got the best of the doctor and he asked why they kept coming back to him. "Well, its this way," the old man said. "I am married and we can't go to my house, and she's married so we can't go to her house. The cost for a motel room is $15.00 so we come here for $10.00 and get $8.00 back from Medicare."

137. A Weekend Pass

Once again we find the familiar theme of old age and diminished sexuality. This joke is also found in oral tradition. For other versions of the joke, see Julius Alvin, *Gross Jokes* (New York: Zebra Books, 1983), p. 95; Blanche Knott, *Truly Tasteless Jokes IV* (New York: Pinnacle Books, 1984), p. 97. The following text was collected in Berkeley in 1980, and it seemingly refers to the onset of a venereal disease.

Never Try to Teach a Pig to Sing

THIS NINETY YEAR OLD MAN LIVED IN A REST HOME
AND GOT A WEEK-END PASS. HE STEPPED INTO HIS
FAVORITE BAR AND SAT DOWN AT THE END AND
ORDERED A DRINK. HE NOTICED A 70 YEAR OLD
WOMAN AT THE OTHER END OF THE BAR AND TOLD
THE BARTENDER TO BUY THE LOVELY LADY A DRINK.
AS THE EVENING PROGRESSED THE OLD MAN JOINED
THE LADY AND THEY WENT TO HER APARTMENT
WHERE THEY GOT IT ON.

FOUR OR FIVE DAYS LATER THE OLD MAN NOTICED
THAT HE WAS DEVELOPING A DRIP, AND HEADED FOR
THE REST HOME DOCTOR. AFTER CAREFUL EXAMINA-
TION THE DOCTOR ASKED THE OLD MAN IF HE HAD
ENGAGED IN SEX RECENTLY. THE OLD MAN SAID
"SURE." THE DOCTOR ASKED IF HE COULD REMEMBER
WHO THE WOMAN WAS AND WHERE SHE LIVED. THE
OLD MAN SAID, "SURE, WHY?" THE DOCTOR REPLIED
"WELL, YOU'D BETTER GET OVER THERE, YOU'RE ABOUT
TO COME."

138. The Damn Things Are Growing Wild

In this exemplar of old age and sexuality, the central character
is a woman. The chronological organization of the commentaries
is reminiscent of other folk items (cf. items 115 and 126). The following item was collected in Foster City, California, in 1986. For
other versions, see Blanche Knott, *Truly Tasteless Jokes 3* (New
York: Ballantine Books, 1983), p. 113; *Playboy's Party Jokes 7* (New
York: PBJ Books, 1975), p. 38; and Shelli Sonstein, *The Thoroughly
Tasteful Dirty Joke Book* (New York: Stein and Day, 1985), p. 72.
For English versions, see RIF, 115 and RJ, 95. For a version set in
India, see Quentin Caras, *Naughty Jokes to Make You Blush* (Bom-
bay: India Book House, 1985), pp. 103–4.

There is this guy who really takes care of his body. He lifts weights and jogs 5 miles a day.

One morning he looks into the mirror and admires his body. He notices he is really suntanned all over except his penis and he decides to do something about it.

He goes to the beach, completely undresses and buries himself in the sand, except for his penis sticking out.

Two little old ladies are strolling along the beach and one looks down and says, "there really is no justice in this world."

The other little old lady says, "what do you mean?"

The first little old lady says, "Look at that!"

When I was 10 years old, I was afraid of it.

When I was 20 years old, I was curious about it.

When I was 30 years old, I enjoyed it.

When I was 40 years old, I asked for it.

When I was 60 years old, I prayed for it.

When I was 70 years old, I forgot about it.

and now that I am 80, the damn things are growing wild.

139. They Don't Make Mirrors Like They Used To

Another elderly female ponders some of the common afflictions of advancing years. Appropriately enough, the first text was collected in a nursing home in Long Beach, New York, in 1988. The second text was collected in Walnut Creek, California, in February 1990. It has a different title, a different initial paragraph, and a postscript.

Never Try to Teach a Pig to Sing

MY DEAR FRIENDS,

I HAVE BECOME 93 YEARS OLD SINCE I SAW YOU LAST, AND A FEW CHANGES HAVE COME INTO MY LIFE SINCE THEN.

FRANKLY, I HAVE BECOME QUITE A FRIVOLOUS OLD GAL: I AM SEEING FIVE GENTLEMEN EVERY DAY.

AS SOON AS I WAKE UP IN THE MORNING WILL POWER HELPS ME TO GET OUT OF BED, THEN HE LEAVES AND I GO SEE JOHN.

THEN CHARLEY HORSE COMES ALONG AND WHEN HE IS HERE HE TAKES A LOT OF TIME AND ATTENTION, WHEN HE LEAVES ARTHUR RITIS SHOWS UP AND STAYS THE REST OF THE DAY. HE DOESN'T LIKE TO STAY IN ONE PLACE VERY LONG, HE TAKES ME FROM JOINT TO JOINT. AFTER SUCH A BUSY DAY I AM REALLY TIRED AND GLAD TO GO TO BED WITH BEN GAY. WHAT A LIFE. HO HUM!!!!!

EVERYTHING IS FARTHER AWAY THAN IT USED TO BE. IT'S TWICE AS FAR TO THE CORNER AND THEY'VE ADDED A HILL I'VE NOTICED. I HAVE GIVEN UP RUNNING FOR THE BUS, IT LEAVES FASTER THAN IT USED TO. IT SEEMS TO ME THEY ARE MAKING STEPS STEEPER THAN IN THE OLD DAYS AND HAVE YOU NOTICED THE SMALLER PRINT THEY USE IN THE NEWSPAPERS AND TELEPHONE BOOKS? THERE'S NO SENSE IN ASKING ANYONE TO READ ALOUD, EVERYONE SPEAKS IN SUCH A LOW VOICE THAT I CAN HARDLY HEAR THEM. THE MATERIAL IN DRESSES IS GETTING SO SKIMPY. ESPECIALLY AROUND THE WAIST AND HIPS. EVEN PEOPLE ARE CHANGING, THEY ARE SO MUCH YOUNGER THAN THEY USED TO BE WHEN I WAS THEIR AGE. ON THE OTHER HAND, PEOPLE MY OWN AGE ARE SO MUCH OLDER THAN I. I RAN INTO AN OLD FRIEND THE OTHER DAY AND SHE HAD AGED SO MUCH SHE DIDN'T EVEN RECOGNIZE ME. I GOT TO THINKING ABOUT THE POOR THING WHILE I WAS COMBING MY HAIR THIS MORNING AND IN DOING SO, I GLANCED AT MY REFLECTION AND WOULD YOU BELIEVE, THEY DON'T MAKE MIRRORS LIKE THEY USED TO.

Different Strokes for Different Folks

Remember, old folks are worth a fortune, with silver in their hair, gold in their teeth, stones in their kidneys, lead in their feet, and gas in their stomachs.

I have become a little older since I saw you last and a few changes have come into my life since then. Frankly, I have become quite a frivolous old gal. I am seeing five gentlemen every day. As soon as I wake up Will Power helps me get out of bed. Then I go see John. Then Charlie Horse comes along and when he is here he takes a lot of my time and attention. When he leaves, Arthur Ritis shows up and stays the rest of the day. He doesn't like to stay in one place very long, so he takes me from joint to joint. After such a busy day, I am tired and glad to go to bed with Ben Gay. What a life!

P. S. The preacher came to call the other day. He said at my age I should be thinking of the hereafter. I told him, "Oh, I do all the time. No matter where I am, in the parlor, upstairs, in the kitchen or down in the basement, I ask myself 'What am I hereafter?'"

140. For All Those Born before 1945

Nostalgia is often enjoyed by the elderly. Memories of the "good old days" are constantly relived with pleasure. The rate of technological and cultural change in the twentieth century, however, has increased the degree of difference between the life-styles of succeeding generations. Young people tend to forget that many of the conveniences which they take for granted were totally unknown to their parents or grandparents. We still refer to a refrigerator as an ice box, but ice is no longer delivered to homes in most American communities. Along with rapid changes in technology has been inflation. The penny postcard is but a memory along with the five-cent cigar.

An interesting overview cataloguing some of the dramatic changes that have occurred in the twentieth century is contained in the following item collected in Santa Cruz, California, in 1989.

FOR ALL THOSE BORN BEFORE 1945

WE ARE THE SURVIVORS!!!
CONSIDER THE CHANGES WE HAVE WITNESSED!!!

. . . .

We were born before television, before penicillin, before polio shots, frozen foods, Xerox, plastic, contact lenses, Frisbees, and "THE PILL". We were before radar, credit cards, split atoms, laser beams, and ballpoint pens. Before pantyhose, dishwashers, clothes dryers, electric blankets, air conditioners, drip-dry clothes . . . and before man walked on the moon.

We got married first and <u>then</u> lived together. How quaint can you be??? In our time, closets were for clothes, not for "coming out of". Bunnies were small rabbits, and rabbits were not Volkswagens. Designer Jeans were scheming girls named Jean, and having a meaningful relationship meant getting along with our <u>cousins.</u>
We thought fast food was what you ate during lent, and "Outer Space" was the back of the Rio Theater. We were before house husbands, gay rights, computer dating, dual careers and commuter marriages. We were before day-care centers, group therapy, and nursing homes. We never heard of FM radio, tape decks, electric typewriters, artificial hearts, word processors, yogurt ice cream and guys wearing earrings. For us, time-sharing meant togetherness . . . not computers or condominiums. A chip meant a piece of wood. Hardware meant hardware, and software wasn't even a word.

Back then, "Made in Japan" meant <u>junk</u> and the term "making out" referred to how you did on your exam. Pizzas, McDonald's, and instant coffees were unheard of. We hit the scene where there were five and dime stores, where you bought things for five and ten cents.

Creamery and Woolworth's sold ice cream cones for a nickel, for one dime you would ride a street car, make a phone call, buy a Pepsi or enough stamps to mail one letter <u>and</u> two postcards. You could buy a new Chevy coupe for $600 . . . but who could afford one? A pity too, because gas was only <u>eleven cents</u> a gallon!

In our days, GRASS was mowed, COKE was a cold drink, and POT was something you cooked in. ROCK MUSIC was Grandma's lullaby and AIDS were helpers in the Principal's Office. We were certainly not before the difference between the sexes was discovered, but we were surely before the sex change. We made do with what the Good Lord blessed us with. And we were the last generation that was so dumb to think you <u>needed</u> a husband to have a baby.

No wonder we are so confused and there is such a generation gap today.

BUT, . . . WE SURVIVED!!!
WHAT BETTER REASON TO CELEBRATE?

. . . .

141. How Can You Tell

The following text, collected in Raleigh, North Carolina, in 1988, presents an alleged stereotype of a salesman. Salesmen frequently have to exaggerate the merits of their product as part of their "sales pitch" in order to successfully sell their quota (and earn commissions). However, the joke in oral tradition more commonly refers to lawyers, not salesmen.

How can you tell

when a salesman is lying?

His Lips Move.

142. When I Was Born, I Was Black

Racial stereotypes often contain references to color. The word "Negro," one must remember, is supposedly from the Spanish or Portuguese term for the color black. In the United States, one term designating Afro-Americans in vogue around the turn of the century was "Colored." In the 1960s, young militant Afro-Americans definitely insisted upon the use of the term "Black" as opposed to "Negro" or "Colored." It was at that time that the statement "Black is beautiful" became popular as part of racial pride. Whatever the term employed, it is a mark of oppression all over the world when a people is forced to take a term from their oppressors as their basic identity label. Why should American Indians, for example, have to accept such labels as Nez Perce, French for pierced nose? Or why even the term Indians for that matter?

In any event, the following item collected from Ripon, California, in 1988, attempts to fight back. An expurgated version of the item appeared in an Ann Landers column in the *Contra Costa Times* for Thursday, February 9, 1989 (p. 8c). For an interesting historical discussion of the terminology for Afro-Americans, see H. L. Mencken, "Designations for Colored Folk," *American Speech* 19 (1944), 161–74, reprinted in Alan Dundes, ed., *Mother Wit from the Laughing Barrel: Readings in the Interpretation of Afro-American Folklore* (Jackson: University Press of Mississippi, 1990), pp. 142–55.

ME

WHEN I WAS BORN — I WAS BLACK

WHEN I GREW UP — I WAS BLACK

WHEN I AM SICK — I AM BLACK

WHEN I GO OUT IN THE SUN — I AM BLACK

WHEN I GO OUT IN THE COLD — I AM BLACK

WHEN I DIE — I AM BLACK

BUT YOU!!!

WHEN YOU ARE BORN — YOU ARE PINK

WHEN YOU GROW UP — YOU ARE WHITE

WHEN YOU ARE SICK — YOU ARE GREEN

WHEN YOU GO OUT IN THE SUN — YOU ARE RED

WHEN YOU GO OUT IN THE COLD — YOU ARE BLUE

WHEN YOU DIE — YOU ARE PURPLE

AND YOU HAVE THE FUCKING NERVE TO CALL ME

"COLORED"!!!!!!!!!

Different Strokes for Different Folks

143. Is This Test Too Tough?

Taking tests is a routine part of American life from earliest childhood through adulthood. Some tests are fair attempts to gauge the amount of knowledge or ability an individual has attained; others seem arbitrary and unrelated to any rational measure of intelligence or aptitude.

The following folk parody of a management test collected from the staff bulletin board of a library in Lafayette, California, in 1987, is more commonly found as part of an entire booklet in large format with such titles as "The Polish (or Irish) Book of Games You Can't Lose." Our second text, from Greensboro, North Carolina, in the early 1980s, consists of a representative booklet with the pages reduced somewhat in size for presentation here. For a consideration of the Polish-American stereotype as manifested in joke cycles, see Alan Dundes, *Cracking Jokes* (Berkeley: Ten Speed Press, 1987), pp. 115–42.

IS THIS TEST TOO TOUGH?

MANAGEMENT TEST

Three or more correct answers could lead you to a promising management position

Can you guess the animal in this incomplete drawing?

Get through the maze.

Connect the dots.

Find the aardvark hiding in the back of the pickup.

THE POLISH BOOK OF GAMES YOU CAN'T LOSE!

CONNECT THE DOTS!

● 1

● 2

WORD SEARCH

Find the word in the word list by looking across, down, diagonally, forwards or backwards. Circle the word you find.

cat

WORD LIST
cat

FIND THE ELEPHANT

can you find the elephant hidden in the picture?

Never Try to Teach a Pig to Sing

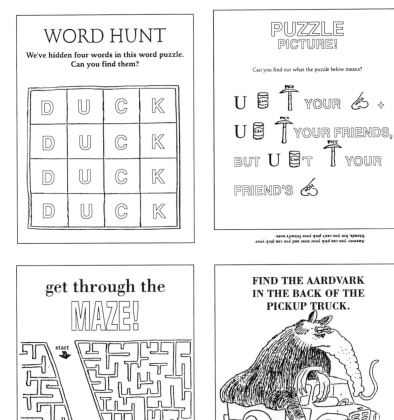

WORD HUNT

**We've hidden four words in this word puzzle.
Can you find them?**

D	U	C	K
D	U	C	K
D	U	C	K
D	U	C	K

PUZZLE PICTURE!

Can you find out what the puzzle below means?

U [CAN] [PICK] YOUR ✏ +

U [CAN] [PICK] YOUR FRIENDS,

BUT U [CAN]'T [PICK] YOUR

FRIEND'S ✏

**Answer: you can pick your nose and you can pick your
friends, but you can't pick your friend's nose.**

get through the MAZE!

start

finish

FIND THE AARDVARK IN THE BACK OF THE PICKUP TRUCK.

There is an Aardvark hiding in the back of this
pickup truck. Can you find him?

How many Honkies
are in this picture?
Find out how many honkies there are in the picture below.

WHICH ONE IS DIFFERENT?

In each of the groups below can you tell which object is different. Try your skill.

COUNT YOUR NOSE

How many noses do you have? Can you find out? Count your nose with your forefinger and write your answer below.

How many noses do you have 1___ 2___ 3___

ANSWER:one

Never Try to Teach a Pig to Sing

It should be noted that no two "editions" of "The Polish Book of Games" are identical, proof positive of their folkloristic nature. Four pages from a so-called "Polish Aptitude Test" collected at a life insurance office in Sacramento in 1983 are presented below (in reduced size) to illustrate some of the interesting variety in this item.

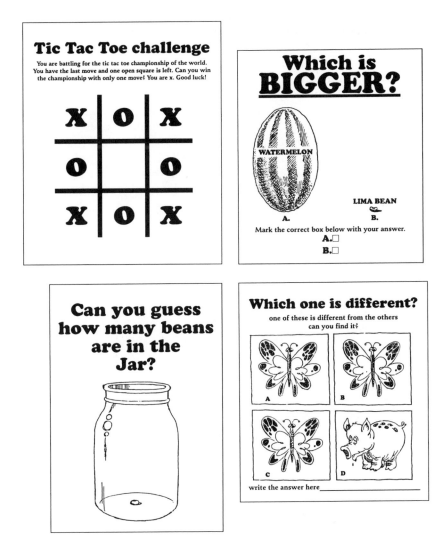

Tic Tac Toe challenge

You are battling for the tic tac toe championship of the world. You have the last move and one open square is left. Can you win the championship with only one move? You are x. Good luck!

X	O	X
O		O
X	O	X

Which is BIGGER?

WATERMELON

LIMA BEAN

A.   B.

Mark the correct box below with your answer.

A.☐

B.☐

Can you guess how many beans are in the Jar?

Which one is different?

one of these is different from the others can you find it?

A   B

C   D

write the answer here_____

144. The Polish (Italian, Irish) Gas Chamber

The use of poison gas in war has been banned by most industrialized nations. The nefarious employment of gas chambers in the incomprehensibly horrendous Nazi death camps would seemingly have made the subject an unlikely one for humor. On the other hand, in the United States where capital punishment is still authorized, the gas chamber remains as one of a small number of sanctioned methods of execution.

In the following ethnic slurs, the gas in question stems from flatulence. Presumably the punishment in these chambers is not lethal but merely unpleasant and malodorous. The first was collected from northern Indiana in 1985; the second from Berkeley in the mid-1980s. The third was collected in Carmel Valley, California, in 1989. The reference to Mount Etna, an active volcano, in the second version, suggests an equivalence between volcanic eruption and flatulence. Versions 2 and 3 are closely related but clearly far from identical.

POLISH GAS CHAMBER

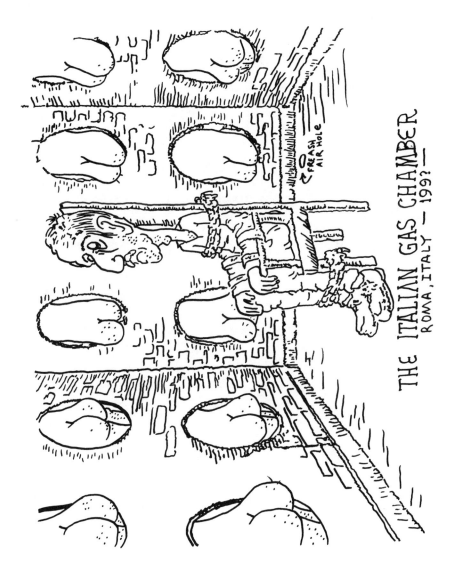

THE ITALIAN GAS CHAMBER
— ROMA, ITALY — 199? —

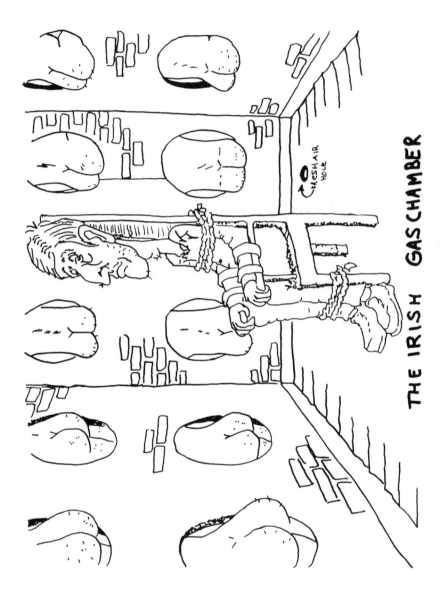

THE IRISH GAS CHAMBER

145. Two Polacks Shooting Crap!

The folk have managed to make an outrageous pun on the dice term "shooting craps" and a common slang synonym for feces. The version below was collected in Clairton, Pennsylvania, in 1976. For another version in which the caption reads "Two North Dakotans Shootin' Crap!" see UFFC-PC, 17.

146. The Italian (Polish) Shower

Another illustration of ethnic bathroom humor has to do with a shower rather than a toilet. Actually, urine can be used as a cleansing agent and is so used by various peoples around the world. Even in the United States, one folk medical practice involves the use of urine to cure sore eyes. (See superstition number 1359 in *The Frank C. Brown Collection of North Carolina Folklore*, Vol. VI [Durham: Duke University Press, 1961], p. 180.) This use of urine might possibly explain the appearance of a commercial eyewash which could be construed as containing the word in the product's name: Murine. Other uses of urine as a cleansing agent include the elimination of freckles (superstition number 1485, p. 194) and the cure of erysipelas (superstition number 1349, p. 179), commonly called "St. Anthony's Fire."

Of course, in the ethnic slur context, urine and feces are regarded as dirty, defiling elements. Smell is commonly used as a part of ethnic slur stereotypes. The first version was collected near Sacramento in 1978 while the second was reported in Kokomo, Indiana, in 1976. For a variant, captioned "Italian shower," see UFFC-PC, 22; for an English non-ethnic variant entitled "Save Water!" see RIF, 67.

ITALIAN SHOWER

POLISH SHOWER

Never Try to Teach a Pig to Sing

147. Imported Wood Stove

Wood stoves are, of course, stoves which burn wood as fuel. Evidently, the Italian and Polish stereotypes have interpreted "wood stove" literally. One should keep in mind that the 1970s saw an international oil cartel in effect which raised prices substantially and cut production. This created an energy shortage in the United States and elsewhere. Individuals began looking feverishly for alternative energy sources. The wood-burning stove quickly became very popular, especially in areas where wood was in plentiful supply.

The first text was collected in San Rafael, California, in 1978; the second from Greensboro, North Carolina, in the early 1980s.

FOR SALE

NEW WOOD STOVE
(IMPORTED FROM ITALY)
MADE OF 'REAL' WOOD.

EXCLUSIVE U.S. AGENT

HURRY!
WHILE THEY
LAST

GUARANTEED
TO BURN AT LEAST
4 HOURS.

Imported from Poland
WOOD STOVE

PATENT PENDING IN PRINCIPAL COUNTRIES OF THE WORLD

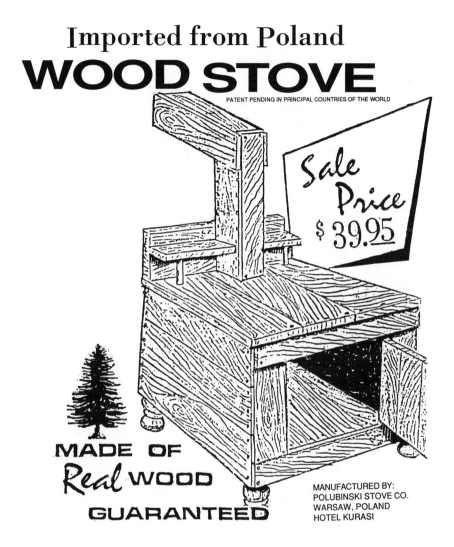

Sale Price $ 39.95

MADE OF
Real WOOD
GUARANTEED

MANUFACTURED BY:
POLUBINSKI STOVE CO.
WARSAW, POLAND
HOTEL KURASI

148. Italian Apple Crate

Still another exercise in construction futility involves an apple crate. In the following cartoon collected in San Francisco in 1976, we see a most unusual design for a box. Aside from the fact that it would hardly hold apples (or most anything else), its peculiar method of attaching the vertical boards reveals the utter absurdity of the structure. Viewed from any angle, the crate's design is flawed.

BUILD AN ITALIAN
APPLE CRATE.

149. Late One Afternoon at a Portuguese Dike

Although the Polish-American and the Italian-American are perhaps the primary targets for ethnic slurs in the late twentieth century, other groups are sometimes the victims. In some parts of the United States where there are Portuguese communities, one may find anti-Portuguese slurs. One such slur was collected in Sacramento in 1979. While dikes are more commonly associated with Holland, they do exist in California. In this instance, the Portuguese individual bravely seeks to plug the hole in the dike with his finger, but he foolishly elects to do so from the underwater side of the wall.

A second item, also illustrating the anti-Portuguese slur tradition, plays linguistically on the name of a prominent Japanese motorcycle manufacturer, Kawasaki. It was collected from a United Parcel Service employee in June 1990, in rural Tulare County, California.

Never Try to Teach a Pig to Sing

PORTUGUESE
MOTORCYCLE

COWASOCKY

150. Dallas Cowboys Schedule

Professional football enjoys immense popularity during the fall season in the United States. For many years, the Dallas Cowboys were a perennial power in the National Football League. Claiming the unoffical title of "America's team," the Cowboys were consistently among the top three or four teams contending for the Super Bowl championship playoffs. In the mid-1980s, the team suddenly fell on hard times and had losing seasons, failing to make the playoffs. Distraught Dallas fans, long accustomed to a winning football program in their city, did not take kindly to the change of fortune of their team. The following parody, collected in Dallas in 1988, suggests a series of opponents not normally considered appropriate for a good high school team, much less a vaunted professional club. The closing platitude belies the deep feelings of football fans for whom winning is everything.

A second version, collected in early 1990 in St. Charles, Missouri, features the Denver Broncos, another professional football team. In contrast to the Dallas Cowboys, the Broncos of late have had very successful winning records. However, despite several appearances in the Super Bowl, the Broncos have yet to win that championship. Presumably this is why the Broncos were deemed an appropriate team for such an unusual schedule.

The two versions are clearly related, but display marked differences. For example, the second version includes homosexual slurs not found in the first version. For a discussion of football as a homosexual ritual, see Alan Dundes, "The American Game of 'Smear the Queer' and the Homosexual Component of Male Competitive Sport and Warfare," in Alan Dundes, *Parsing through Customs: Essays by a Freudian Folklorist* (Madison: University of Wisconsin Press, 1987), pp. 178–94.

Dallas Cowboys
Schedule
1987

Sept. 7	North Dallas Jr. High	Away
Sept. 14	Cub Scout Troop 101	Home
Sept. 21	Texas Blind Academy	Home
Oct.5	Spanish-American War Vets	Away
Oct.12	Crippled Children's Home	Home
Oct. 19	Girl Scout Troop 679	Away
Nov. 2	Van Horn Boy's Choir	Away
Nov. 9	Korean War Amputees	Home
Nov. 16	Polio Patients Assn.	Away

RULE CHANGES FROM LAST YEAR

★ When playing Polio Patients, the Cowboys must not disconnect their leg braces.

★ When playing the Blind Academy the Cowboys must not hide the ball under their jerseys.

★ All Cowboy touchdowns will count 21 points.

★ The Cowboys will be allowed 14 men on the field at all times.

★ The Cowboys will be allowed 20 time-outs each half.

★ The Cowboys will be awarded a first down with each gain of 3 yards.

"IT'S NOT WHETHER YOU WIN OR LOSE, IT'S HOW YOU PLAY THE GAME"

DENVER BRONCOS
1990
FOOTBALL SCHEDULE

SEPT.14----LITTLE SISTERS OF THE POOR
SEPT.21----CUB SCOUT PACK #122
SEPT.28----COLORADO HOME OF THE BLIND
OCT. 5----SPANISH-AMERICAN WAR VETERANS
OCT. 12----PUEBLO HOME FOR CRIPPLED CHILDREN
OCT. 19----BUCKS COUNTRY HOME FOR UNWED
          MOTHERS
OCT. 26----GIRL SCOUT TROOP #235
NOV. 2----COLORADO SPRINGS V.D. CLINIC #69
NOV. 10----NEW HOPE BOYS CHOIR
NOV. 16----KOREAN WAR AMPUTEES
NOV. 23----V.A. HOSPITAL POLIO VICTIMS

SPECIAL MONDAY NIGHT GAME

DEC. 1----FORT COLLINS HOME FOR GAYS

RULE CHANGES FROM LAST YEAR

#1 When playing polio patients, BRONCOS must not discon-
nect leg braces.
#2 When playing the GIRL SCOUTS, keep your hands off their
cookies.
#3 When playing the HOME FOR THE BLIND, do not hide the
ball.
#4 When playing the GAYS, protect your ass at all times.

NAME CHANGE

The DENVER BRONCOS will hereafter be referred to as the
DENVER TAMPONS, since they are only good for one period
and they have no second string.

COACHES CHANGE

DAN REEVES will be replaced by LINDA LOVELACE. She
will no doubt blow a few, but she won't choke on the big ones.

Never Try to Teach a Pig to Sing

151. "Looks Like It's Going to be a Great Year"

For a long time, racism in professional sports kept Black players from participating. Even now that professional baseball, football, and basketball teams do have large numbers of Black athletes on their rosters, the leadership positions, e.g., quarterbacks, coaches, managers, are still rarely filled by Blacks. Fortunately, the situation appears to be changing albeit at a very slow pace.

After years of ignoring talented Black athletes, coaches even at previously all-white southern schools are engaged in a veritable recruiting war to attract the best prospects to their campuses. The desire of some institutions to mount a championship team has encouraged the recruitment of individuals lacking the usual minimum academic qualifications for college. The failure of some educational institutions to support these athletes outside of the sports program has resulted in an extremely low rate of graduation among many of these minority students.

The following racist item parodies college recruiting efforts. The version presented here was collected in Oakland in 1985. Other versions are nominally attributed to the University of North Carolina and the University of California, Berkeley. A published version in *Maledicta 9* (1986–87), 37–38, refers to the University of Wisconsin and mentions other versions from the University of Minnesota and the University of Miami.

NOT FOR PUBLIC RELEASE

PROSPECTIVE 1983 HOUSTON BASKETBALL SIGNEE'S
    TO DATE

WOODROW ALSOTON—6'8"—198 lbs. Lives in Amherst, but born in the Bronx where mother was on welfare the last 20 years. At 19, he is the oldest of 10 children, all illegitimate. Expensive tastes—wants two mink coats and purple Cadillac to sign. WILL PROBABLY GET THEM.

ROOSEVELT "DUDE" DANZELL—6'6"—215 lbs. Halfbreed from West Virginia. Has processed hair and thinks he's Billy Dee Williams. Biggest drawback—very light skinned and, therefore, snubbed by teammates. Considering a lower lip transplant in order to be accepted by peers.

LEOTIS B. JENKINS, JR.— 6'4"— 192 lbs. Tappenhannock High— very fast and above average intelligence. Only member of his team who knows his father. Spells name without assistance. Likes white wimmin, white likkor, and white ice cream, in that order. Led his high school in rebounds; also led burglary attempts at Harry's One Stop Stereo Shop. Got 5 to 10 years, served 6 days. NOW OUT AND READY TO PLAY.

MARVIN Z. PALAFOX— 7'2"— 195 lbs. White, but doesn't know the difference. Insists on wearing number 12. Scored same on College Boards. Thinks Sherlock Holmes is a housing development. Loves buttermilk, but can't spell it. Ugly as hell, makes Junior Sample look like Robert Redford. BEDWETTER.

WILLIE "TRAIN" GREEN— 6'6"— 200 lbs. Point guard. Born on Amtrack near Baltimore, as mother was hoping to make it to Philly to enhance welfare benefits. Missed half his senior season— terminal acne. He'll hit you under the basket say recruiters, especially if you call him ZIT HEAD!!

REMARQUE WINEGLASS— 6'7"— 188 lbs. Pulaski's finest prospect in a decade. Musically inclined, wants mini-cassette installed in headband so he can run the fast-breaks to "Commodore". Holds regional record for interview "You know"s 62 over a one minute, 10 second span!! Wants buckets of cash for his "X" on dotted line. Contact thru his agent, Sam the Fly, at the Wise Owl Pool Hall.

ALBERT WARTZ— 6'11"— 200 lbs. Only other white prospect, but totally stupid. Thinks Henry Cabot Lodge is a Charlotteville Motel. Great hands say the coaches, SO DO THE CHEERLEADERS. When filling out questionnaire, by "sex" he wrote "NOT SINCE MAVIS WILSON LEFT TOWN".

ABBA BWANAIKA— 7'7"— 235 lbs. Zulu tribesman, age unknown. Teeth indicate about 24 years old. Recommended by alumnus serving the dark continent in Peace Corps. Spent early years in tree house. Unmarried— 6 children. Also known as "POOTIE". Has not bathed in over a year. Requires separate transportation to and from games.

COACH'S REMARK AT EVALUATION MEETING—
"LOOKS LIKE IT'S GOING TO BE A GREAT YEAR".

152. Appeal Upheld

Although many states in the United States do still authorize capital punishment, the eighth amendment of the United States Constitution expressly forbids the infliction of "cruel and unusual punishments." Earlier western justice based upon *lex talionis* did permit an eye for an eye and in some parts of the contemporary Arab world, such forms of punishment are still permitted. Thus, in theory, a thief might have his hand cut off. This provides an opportunity for the folk to comment on their perception of Arab justice, and they do so in the following cartoon collected in Oakland in 1984. Implicit also is the awareness of the possible limitations of Western legal procedures in other cultural contexts. In this instance, the futility of appeal is obvious.

153. Dear Earthling

Even though most of us have never met an extraterrestrial being, we still hold stereotypes of such creatures, thanks in part to
science fiction writings and films. The fact that the content of the
following items deals with unusual sexual behavior is obviously
a reflection of our own cultural fixation. It is also of interest that
the extraterrestrial knows how to communicate in letter format
and in English! (as opposed to all the other languages spoken on
the face of the earth!). It was collected in Napa, California in 1988.
A second text was collected in Gaithersburg, Maryland, in the
1970s. For an English parallel to the first text, see RIF, 127.

Dear Earthling,

**Hi! I am a creature from outer
space. I have transformed myself
into this piece of paper. Right now
I am having sex with your fingers.
I know you like it because you are
smiling. Please pass me on to
someone else because I'm really
horny.**

Thanks!

I'm from outer space. My sex
organs are in my thumb. We
have just had sexual intercourse. If you enjoyed it—
S M I L E !

154. Take Me to Your Leader

If we are at all confused about the appearance of extraterres-
trials, we can also imagine that they might be confused about objects on earth. The following folk cartoon from Altrincham, Cheshire, England, in 1977 plays on a possible misconception on the part
of an alien visitor to our planet. Evidently, the alien society has a
similar hierarchic structure to human society. For another English
text, see RIF, 77.

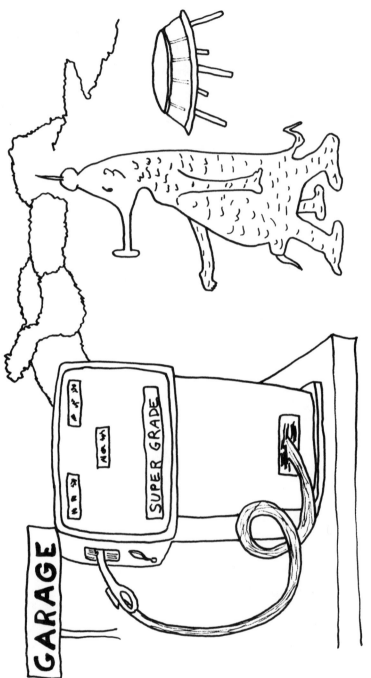

TAKE ME TO YOUR LEADER AND TAKE YOUR DICK OUT OF YOUR EAR WHEN YOU SPEAK TO AN OFFICER.

155. Oh What a Beautiful Morning

Sometimes humans encounter creatures already on this earth rather than alien visitors. In this case, a cute bug, full of optimism and good spirit, sings a song from the hit musical comedy "Oklahoma!" Instead of singing the final portion of the chorus, "Everything's going my way," the bug encounters man. In the world of bugs, man may be god. But as the bug is, so also is man with respect to his god or fate. This cartoon was collected in Oakland in 1977. For an English version of this sequence, see RIF, 76.

156. I'll Have the Gazpacho

An insect with considerably more sophistication encounters a different sort of human, a true gourmet who clearly enjoys elegant dining. The detail of the drawing and the wording of the text suggest the work of a professional cartoonist. However, none of our versions bear any indication of authorial ascription. The version here was collected in Oakland in 1981, but our earliest version dates from 1977. A version published in *Maledicta* 5 (1981), 126, is accompanied by a note stating that the cartoon appeared in *National Lampoon* the same year.

The humor comes in part from the stark contrast between the urbane and the crude, the man and a human-sized fly as dinner companions. Another opposition is between food and feces. Perhaps there is also an implied criticism of the excessive snobbery of food fetishists.

Quick on the Draw:
Folk Cartoons

There can be no doubt that no form of photocopier folklore is more popular than the folk cartoon. Chapters devoted to the folk cartoon in both *Work Hard and You Shall Be Rewarded* (WH) and *When You're Up to Your Ass in Alligators . . .* (WY) did not by any means exhaust the rich variety of materials actively circulating. Some of the folk cartoons we have been able to trace back several decades, but others appear to be newly created. What is truly remarkable about these folk cartoons is that they are unquestionably re-drawn. While one might think that the office copier would tend to inhibit re-creating folk cartoons, the indisputable evidence of multiple existence with variation proves otherwise. We have tried in a number of instances to document this variation by providing at least two examples of specific folk cartoons.

157. As Seen By

Any individual may be perceived differently by various persons or groups. These perceptions may demonstrate considerable variation. A traditional cartoon sequence illustrates this. The first exemplar collected in Winnipeg in 1980 depicts a salesman, while the second version from Knoxville, Tennessee, in 1977 refers to a scientist. The style of drawing of both cartoons suggests a much earlier date of origin of the sequence. Noteworthy in the sequence is the literalization of the folk metaphor "to be a horse's ass," meaning someone who is a jackass, that is, someone who makes a fool of himself, or someone who has an inflated high opinion of himself.

A third text from Menlo Park, California, in 1990 demonstrates how one's house is envisioned differently "as seen by" one's lender, buyer, appraiser, and the Internal Revenue Service.

For another version, see *Furthermore Over Sexteen*, Vol. 4 (New York: Grayson, 1956), p. 47. For a variant of our third text, see YD [171].

THE SALESMAN--AS SEEN BY:

HIS BOSS

HIS WIFE

HIS CUSTOMERS

HIS COMPETITORS

DEADWOOD · WORRIES · OVERWORK

HIMSELF

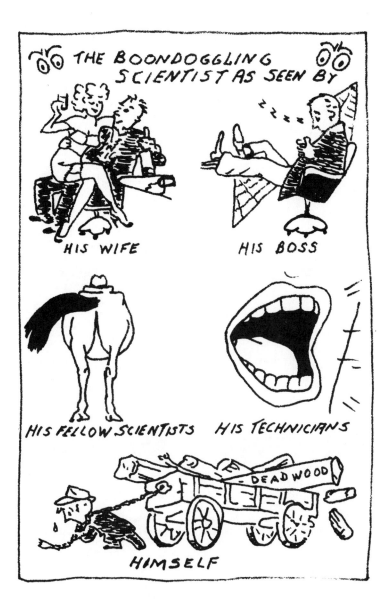

158. We Have Read Your Proposal

The difference between the ideal and the real, between form and substance, is a favorite theme in office-copier folklore. The form letter acknowledging receipt of a proposal is typically polite and courteous. The folk cartoon collected from the office wall of a proposal editor of a company located in Washington, D.C., in 1979 suggests to the contrary that the proposal is not being given serious consideration at all. In fact, the proposal is evidently a source of great amusement if not unrestrained hysterical laughter. (The cartoon also reflects the anxiety felt by most if not all proposal writers who fear that what they consider a legitimate plan or request may be ridiculed by their peers or superiors.)

For another version, see OHB, 15. The true reaction to the proposal is strongly reminiscent of another folk cartoon reported earlier in *When You're Up to Your Ass in Alligators . . .* entitled "You Want It *When?*" (item 93, p. 167) in which a request for immediate action causes riotous hilarity.

WE HAVE READ YOUR PROPOSAL
AND ARE GIVING IT SERIOUS CONSIDERATION.

159. Poor Cynthia

Absenteeism can be a serious problem for businesses, large and small. Sick leave, which is supposed to be reserved for periods of illness, is sometimes used by employees for personal reasons rather than sickness. On the other hand, sometimes there are pressing reasons why an individual may be unable to come to work. The following folk cartoon collected from a secretary at Highland Elementary School in Oakland in 1980 shows to what imaginary lengths a person might go to request time off once the authorized sick leave quota has been exhausted. For a version published in England, see RJ, 80.

"Poor Cynthia. She used up all her sick leave, so she had to call in dead this morning."

Never Try to Teach a Pig to Sing

160. What Did the Boss Have to Say?

The metaphor of an employee's being chewed out by his boss is common in cartoon form. The first version was collected in Irvine, California, in 1976; the second in Oakland in 1980; the third again from Irvine in 1989; the fourth from Costa Mesa, California, in 1976. (For two versions of our fourth example, see UFFC-PC, 130–31; for another see, RJ, 16.) A fifth item from Oakland in 1974 uses a slightly different metaphor, namely, "losing one's ass" e.g., at games of chance. For another version, see YD [113]. For a text with the caption "Well how'd you make out with the old man?" but with a different cartoon (the one with a man with a screw through him, exiting from the company president's office), see *Over Sexteen* (New York: Elgart, 1951), p. 73. The cartoon is in fact an early version of "Work Hard and You Shall Be Rewarded" (cf. WH, pp. 145–53).

CARTOON of the MONTH

"*What did the Boss have to say?*"

NOTHING SERIOUS...

JUST A LITTLE CHAT WITH THE BOSS!!

Nothing serious

Just a little chat with the Boss!!!

Never Try to Teach a Pig to Sing

"How did you do at Las Vegas...?"

161. First Aid

Employees who do not "move" fast enough to suit their bosses may be told to "get the lead out." The literalization of this metaphor provides the raw material for a cartoon which has been in active circulation for more than a quarter of a century. No doubt one reason for the popularity of this particular cartoon is its treatment of a type of medical examination which often causes embarrassment to a patient. The first version was collected in San Francisco in 1950; the second was in circulation in Oakland in 1975 but dates from 1955; the third from ISR was collected at the Chicago Police Department in 1961. (For another version, see *More Over Sexteen* [New York: Grayson, 1953], p. 51.

Never Try to Teach a Pig to Sing

162. I Said a Butt Light

Another folk cartoon involving a proctological examination involves a play on an advertising commercial for Budweiser Light beer. A series of television commercials in the late 1980s featured a mistaken response to a request for a "Bud Light," meaning a bottle or glass of Budweiser Light beer. Typically, the customer asks the bartender for a "light," not specifying Budweiser in particular. As if by magic, a bright glaring light appears, often a dangerous incendiary one. The chastened customer learns to ask for "Bud Light" by name. The folk cartoon offers a reversal of the advertisement insofar as a nurse is shown presenting a bottle of beer (presumably Budweiser) to a proctologist who alters the punch line of the commercial "I said Bud Light" to scold her for not bringing a proctoscope.

I SAID A BUTT Light

163. Go Right Ahead

The metaphor of being "dumped on" is a common expression of rejection in American culture (cf. item 130 above). Someone who feels he or she is constantly put upon can easily identify with the resigned acceptance of the figure in the following cartoon. The first version was found in circulation at Hughes Aircraft Company in El Segundo, California, in 1968. The second version was collected in Washington, D.C., in 1973. For another version, see *Over Sexteen* (New York: Elgart, 1951), p. 69.

Go right ahead - everyone else does

164. The Boss Has Spoken!!

If employees fear being dumped on, then presumably the one who they fear will do the dumping is their superior, that is, the boss. The idea that one's boss is an asshole, meaning a pompous nonentity, would follow logically from this. (This common meaning of "asshole" is inexplicably absent from Harold Wentworth and Stuart Berg Flexner's *Dictionary of American Slang* [New York: Thomas Y. Crowell, 1967]). For a traditional elaborate delineation of the boss as asshole, see WH, 100–101.

In the following cartoon, passing wind is equated to a speech act. Actually, wind is often used to refer to types of speaking. A person who is extremely verbose and perhaps pretentious as well may be termed "long-winded" or a "windbag." Such a person might also be said to be "full of hot air." In the same way, "gas" (related to gastrointestinal?) appears in comparable idioms. One "passes gas" (a euphemism for flatulence), and gas also means empty talk or *in*flated speech. A gasbag is an old term for a braggart or long-winded orator. An "old fart" might be someone well on in years who talks too much. Since flatus is defined in most dictionaries as *gas* in the stomach or intestines, the use of "gas" confirms the equivalence of flatulence and a speech act.

In storytelling, a "windy" is an alternate term for tall tale and "to shoot the breeze" means to gossip or talk idly in a group context. Lest we ourselves be guilty of what we are describing, we shall herewith end this airy disquisition by observing that creation by anal means has been suggested as a male technique intended to compete with female procreativity. Thus, even a male God functioning as a prime mover may take the form of a divine (af)flatus, perhaps moving upon the surface of the primeval waters. For further discussion of this controversial notion, see Alan Dundes, "Earth-Diver: Creation of the Mythopoeic Male," *American Anthropologist* 64 (1962), 1032–51, and "A Psychoanalytic Study of the Bullroarer," *Man* 11 (1976), 220–38. For more on the folklore of farting, see Legman, NLM, 858–90; Alfred Limbach, *Der Furz* (Koln: Argos Press, 1980); Bob Burton Brown, *Common Scents: The First Book of Farts* (Gainsville: Moosebec Press, 1982); and Colin Spencer and Chris Barlas, *Reports from Behind* (London: Enigma Books, 1984).

The following version was collected in Buffalo in 1977. In other versions (not presented here), no man appears and instead of the boss, a political figure is mentioned, Lyndon Baines Johnson for example. (See UFFC-PC, 76). Politicians to be successful must be outspoken, that is, they must speak out about important issues. Sometimes speaking out consists of "raising a stink" about an incumbent's policies, a metaphor not unrelated to the present discussion.

Never Try to Teach a Pig to Sing

165. Please Keep Your Ass Off My Desk!

In most offices, employees have a designated area they may call their own. It may be a small cubicle or it may be just a desk, but whatever the size, it takes on the dimensions of personal space. That personal space may become so important to its occupant that any violation of it by another employee may be regarded as an affront. The following folk cartoon collected at Bechtel Corporation in San Francisco in 1977 presents a pleasant warning to potential trespassers.

166. I Assume That This Is a Refusal

Not all forms of rejection are equally polite. We have previously discussed the prevalence of the "kiss my ass" rejoinder (cf. items 117 and 118 above). In the following folk cartoon collected from the Glendale Federal Savings bank in Fullerton, California, in 1988, the response is to a request for a loan. When one realizes that desks can be used as power and distancing symbols by those in authority, one can see that the would-be borrower is being kept at quite a distance from the bank official. The irony of the cartoon is that many savings and loan institutions in the United States ran into serious financial trouble in the late 1980s precisely because they did *not* exercise sufficient restraint in making loans.

"I assume that this is a refusal."

167. I Take It They Don't Like the Treaty

Probably the most common gesture of rejection is the famous finger, the so-called *digitus impudicus*. It is, in fact, the subject of diverse folk cartoons (cf. "The Finger" in WH, 154–56 [also UFFC-PC, 90], and "Old Lady Hitchhiker" in WY, 186–87, as well as "The Last Great Act of Defiance" in WY, 188–91).

In the following cartoon from Kokomo, Indiana, in 1976, the U.S. Cavalry in a fort receives a smoke signal from some American Indians. Historically, the Indians were rarely asked whether or not they liked a particular treaty. Treaties more often than not were simply imposed unilaterally and even then were frequently violated or broken by the U.S. government.

"I take it they don't like the treaty!"

168. I Don't Think They're Coming Down

In this folk cartoon collected in Walnut Creek, California, in 1988, it is the potential prey of the duck hunters who cleverly fly in formation to send a meaningful message in the vernacular to their foe.

Sometimes, the gesture is referred to in words. This is the case in the second item, which was collected in Oakland, California, in March 1990. "Up yours" is an abridged form of "Up your ass" or "Stick it up your ass." See Harold Wentworth and Stuart Berg Flexner, *Dictionary of American Slang* (New York: Thomas Y. Crowell, 1967), pp. 520, 563.

"I don't think they're coming down."

169. I've Forgotten My Wallet

In the following cartoon collected near Knoxville, Tennessee, in 1977, a drunk is apparently unaware of his nakedness. It may be noteworthy that it is man's "lower" self which, metaphorically speaking, is exposed by the influence of alcohol.

CARTOON of the MONTH

"Good grief! I've forgotten my wallet."

170. Did You Fart?

The folklore of farting has already been discussed (cf. item 164 above). In the first folklore cartoon, collected in Buffalo in 1972, the bartender's question is surely rhetorical given the state of the table and chairs and wall. The advertisement for hard-boiled eggs is presumably a reference to the malodorous scent of rotten eggs, that is, the smell of H_2S, hydrogen sulphide, an olfactory equivalent of the results of flatulence. The second cartoon from Altrincham, Cheshire, England, in 1979, expresses the same admiration for a passing acquaintance.

DID YOU FART?

Never Try to Teach a Pig to Sing

171. The Worst Case of Diarrhea

While excessive farting may disturb others, excessive defecation is more of an individual problem. Diarrhea in its most severe form, e.g., through amoebic dysentery, can be life-threatening. Travelers abroad encountering impurities in the local water supply fear their consequences. There are even folk names for the disease: "Montezuma's revenge," "the Mexican two-step," "the runs," "the trots," and the term "turista" (the Latin American term for the ailment.)

The following folk cartoon collected from the cleaning staff of a London police station in 1988 shows an individual clearly *in extremis*. There may also be an implicit critique of the medical profession insofar as the observing physicians in attendance simply comment on the case without rendering any assistance whatsoever to the afflicted sufferer. Patients are often discomfitted when doctors display a purely clinical interest in their condition, that is, as a medical oddity, instead of evincing a personal concern for their welfare. The posture of the two doctors who stand with their hands in their pockets or behind their backs perhaps signals their failure to give a hand to the poor patient. For another English version, see TCB, 119.

Never Try to Teach a Pig to Sing

172. Patience, My Ass!

The teaching of patience is part of childhood socialization. One is taught to wait for the right moment to be given additional privileges, e.g., to date, drink, or drive. Sometimes the plea for patience creates frustration. In this folk cartoon, the irony is that a buzzard, whose role as an eater of carrion requires that he wait to eat until some animal has died or been killed, is the individual who vows to take action. The cartoon and caption have also appeared on children's T-shirts. The first version was collected in Wilmington, Delaware, in 1990, but bearing a date of 1984; the second version was collected in Bismarck, North Dakota, in 1973; the third was found in the Department of German office at the University of California, Berkeley, in 1979. Besides the slight differences in the written text, there is quite substantial variation in the drawings of the vultures. For three additional versions, see UFFC-PC, 92–94; for another, see YD [88]; for an English version, see RIF, 153.

PATIENCE, MY ASS!
I'M GONNA KILL SOMETHING

Never Try to Teach a Pig to Sing

173. The Same Old Bull

One of the most widespread folk terms to denote something which is untrue or vastly exaggerated is "bullshit" sometimes abbreviated "B.S." or euphemized as "bull." The following three items all involve a reference to this term. The first item was collected in Detroit in 1983; the second, which proscribes bullshitting, was collected at the Chabot College branch located in Livermore, California, in 1984; the third item was collected from a cork bulletin board in a conference room at the University of Utah in Salt Lake City in the early 1970s. For a version of the first item, see OHB, 37; for versions of the third item, see YD [61] and RJ, 41.

ARE YOU TIRED OF THE SAME OLD BULL?

COWS MAY COME
AND COWS MAY GO
BUT THE BULL IN THIS PLACE
GOES ON FOREVER.

Never Try to Teach a Pig to Sing

174. Would You Be Terribly Upset?

In large complex organizations, it is often difficult to find the right office or individual to answer a question or solve a problem. Organization charts do not always work and in any case may not be known to outsiders or even to some of those who work within the organization. As a result of not knowing precisely where to direct an inquiry, many people find themselves addressing questions to the wrong persons. These latter individuals may become so annoyed at receiving a constant barrage of questions for which they have no responsibility to answer that they are tempted to respond in a rude manner. As an alternative, they may elect to post in a prominent place the following cartoon notice.

There appear to be two general sub-types of this notice, and we shall present examples of both. The first version was collected from the photocopier machine operator at Lawrence Berkeley Laboratories in 1979. The second was collected in Ripon, California, in 1988. Many versions of this extremely popular item contain a cat which bears a strong resemblance to the American animated cartoon character Sylvester, who speaks with a lisp and who is repeatedly frustrated in his attempt to capture Tweety-Bird, a pet canary. For another version, see YD, 118. In an English version (OHB, 44), a female secretary at a computer work station rather than a cat requests the client to take his "asinine" problem down the hall. For another English version, see TCB, 55.

WOULD YOU BE TERRIBLY UPSET IF I ASKED YOU TO TAKE YOUR SILLY-ASSED PROBLEM DOWN THE HALL ?

Never Try to Teach a Pig to Sing

Would it upset you terribly,
if I asked you to take your
Silly-Ass problem down the hall,
per chance to find Someone
who Really Gives A Shit!

175. Every Day of My Life

There are two distinct meanings associated with the "kiss my ass" metaphor. Telling someone to kiss one's ass is a traditional gesture of defiance and rejection in many parts of the world (cf. items 117 and 118 above). On the other hand, kissing someone's ass or the presumed act of ass-kissing refers to fawning, obsequious behavior by a junior to a senior individual designed to get ahead through ingratiation (cf. WH, 163–64).

An example of the first meaning may be found in the following folk cartoon collected in Morgan Hill, California, in 1987. A Donald Duck-like figure, carrying old-fashioned tools of the engineer's trade, e.g., a T-square and a slide rule, is evidently frustrated by his associates or clients. A second version from Fishersville, Virginia, in 1989, is presented to show the variation in the drawing: cigarette instead of a pipe, a golf club instead of a T-square, different shoe style, length of tail, etc.

A second type of illustration of the rejoinder usage occurs in both wallet card and memo(randum) format. The first version was collected in Oakland in 1976, while the second was collected in San Francisco in 1975. Note that the position of the left hand grasping the right upper arm may suggest that the right arm and hand are engaged in "giving the finger" to the addressee. (For a discussion of this gesture, see items 167 and 168 above.)

A third basic text, entitled "To My Customers," illustrates the second usage of the ass-kissing metaphor. Salesmen are dependent for their living upon remaining in the good graces of their customers. Salesmen who deal repeatedly with the same customers may have to resort to demeaning, servile behavior to maintain favor. This text collected in 1968 in Kokomo, Indiana, protests against the system, but ends reluctantly with an acknowledgment of its necessity. (An older version dated 1959 in ISR is entitled "Notice to Customers.")

As salesmen have to ass-kiss to keep customers happy, so management sometimes feels it has to cater to the whims and wishes of its work force. Originally pressured by the rise of labor unions and collective bargaining, management has had to become increasingly sensitive to the needs and demands of its employees. Even in the absence of strong unions, companies must be concerned about employee morale and well-being to avoid suffering from low productivity, absenteeism, and shortages of employees. Management's resentment at having to act in this fashion is reflected in the following notice collected at the Naval Air Station in Alameda, California, in 1976.

Finally, it is more usual to think of ass-kissing in connection with subordinates kissing superiors' asses rather than the other way around. A last exemplar collected in San Francisco in 1988 demonstrates this more common usage. In this case, the text is clearly a reaction to the outbreak of AIDS. For a parallel to this text, see Reinhold Aman, "Kakologia: A Chronicle of Nasty Riddles and Naughty Wordplays," *Maledicta 9* (1986–87), 292; for another, see RJ, 46.

"EVERY DAY OF MY LIFE FORCES ME TO ADD TO THE NUMBER OF PEOPLE WHO CAN KISS MY ASS!!!"

EVERY DAY OF MY LIFE
FORCES ME TO ADD TO THE
NUMBER OF PEOPLE WHO
CAN KISS MY ASS!

Never Try to Teach a Pig to Sing

MEMO

In Reply To Your Recent Suggestion:

Sincerely,

MEMO

IN REGARDS TO YOUR RECENT MEMO

Quick on the Draw: Folk Cartoons   313

TO MY CUSTOMERS

Due to my independent position as a Salesman, I have decided to limit my time as best suited to my own convenience.

At the present moment, it pleases me to call on you on Tuesdays and Thursdays, between the hours of 2:00 and 4:00 p.m. probably by phone.

This will allow me to start and extend my weekends without interruptions. It will also permit me to devote my mornings to rest and recreations.

Signed:

Salesman

NOTE: The above regulations apply only as long as business is good. After that, I will be around kissing your ass as usual.

ALL EMPLOYEES ARE REQUESTED TO

TAKE A BATH EVERY MORNING

BEFORE REPORTING TO WORK

Since we have to KISS YOUR ASS to get you

to do any work around here, we would like

to have it clean!

The Management

Never Try to Teach a Pig to Sing

DUE TO THE OUTBREAK OF AIDS, EMPLOYEES WILL NO LONGER BE PERMITTED TO KISS THE BOSS'S ASS

176. Behind Mt. Rushmore

Perhaps the most striking sculptured monument in the United States is Mount Rushmore National Memorial located in the Black Hills of South Dakota. It was the work of one dedicated man, Gutzon Borglum (1867–1941), who carved into a huge granite cliff four giant sixty-foot busts of Presidents Washington, Jefferson, Lincoln, and Theodore Roosevelt. This Idaho-born American sculptor began the work in 1927 and continued until his death. The work was completed thereafter by his son Lincoln. It is a major tourist attraction, and it was featured in the climax of the exciting Alfred Hitchcock comedy-thriller *North by Northwest* (1959), starring Cary Grant and Eva Marie Saint.

The following cartoon collected from a Pacific Bell Telephone information operator's office in Pleasanton, California, in 1988, articulates the folk's natural curiosity about objects and events. People often want to know the "inside story" or what goes on *behind* the scenes. The lives of the rich and famous are invariably of interest. Tabloids and television magazine programs may even pander to such curiosity. In this case, the question of what the back of Mount Rushmore looks like is given an imaginative answer.

A second cartoon collected from a Pacific Gas and Electric office in San Francisco in late 1989 offers another comparison between the human buttocks and a topographical feature. In this case, the idiom in question refers to the ultimate in stupidity. Someone unable to distinguish his "ass from a hole in the ground" is truly benighted. The cartoon is a commentary on senior management as well as upon the plethora of simple-minded workshops, seminars, programs, and training sessions for upwardly mobile corporate executives. For another version, see RJ, 7.

...near as I can tell,
we're somewhere
behind Mt. Rushmore

"WELCOME, GENTLEMEN, TO ADVANCED MANAGEMENT TRAINING."

Never Try to Teach a Pig to Sing

177. Your Problem Is Quite Obvious

Another insulting idiom in American folk speech makes reference to a person having his head up his ass. It conveys that the object of the insult is ignorant, oblivious to his situation or surroundings, or just dense. The implication is that the individual so scorned is not using his head properly—he's not thinking, he's not seeing (like the proverbial ostrich who buries his head in the sand when threatened).

We present three versions of a cartoon which literalizes this folk metaphor. The first is from San Fransisco in 1978 (but with indications that it originated in Salt Lake City); the second is from near Sacramento in 1978; the third is from Raleigh, North Carolina, in 1988. The three versions provide a marvelous demonstration of variation in the cartoon character's position. In the first version, the individual's feet are pointed inward with the big toes nearly touching; in the second, the feet are wide apart; in the third, the toes are touching.

The different placement of the hands is even more striking. In the first version, both palms are flat on the ground. In the second version, both hands are resting on the individual's buttocks; in the third version, one hand is on the ground (but palm up) while the other rests on the buttocks. Although the accompanying caption text shows relatively little variation, the size of the type and the format vary considerably. In the first version, the caption is presented horizontally in one line; in the second, the presentation is partly horizontal, partly vertical in two lines; in the third, the caption is essentially vertical in four lines. This is just a sample of the empirically observable differences among the three versions. For two other versions, see UFFC: PC, 98–99; for a different cartoon based on the same metaphor, see "The Italian (Polish) Air-Raid Shelter" in WH, 179.

Your Problem is quite Obvious

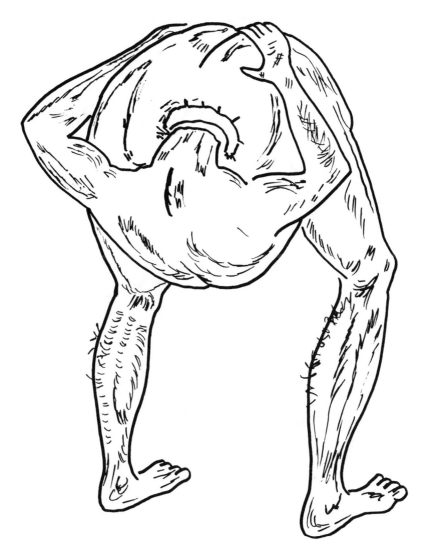

YOUR PROBLEM
IS OBVIOUS

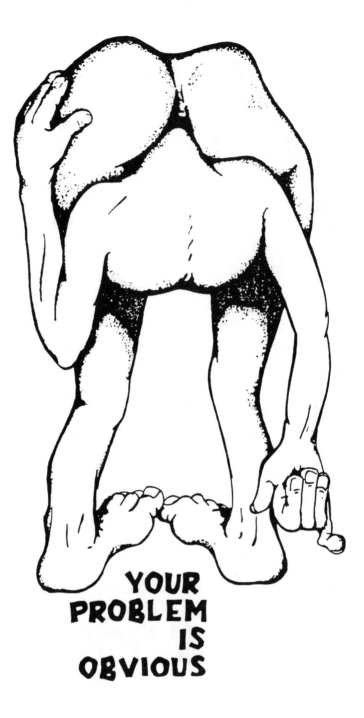

YOUR
PROBLEM
IS
OBVIOUS

Never Try to Teach a Pig to Sing

178. Hey Earl

Another popular derisive term is "asshole." It refers to a person who is a silly fool or a nincompoop, the latter a word whose derivation is admittedly obscure but which almost certainly refers to the same basic posterior area of the human body (cf. the poop or "after" part of a ship, or "poo-poo" as baby talk for feces). The confusion between literal and metaphorical assholes provides the basis for the following folk cartoon sequence collected in Oakland in 1980. The men riding the elephant must really be stupid to think that the commentators on foot are referring to elephantine anatomy.

For another version, see UFFC-PC, 52; for a narrative version involving a camel rather than an elephant, see Jackie Martling, *The Only Dirty Joke Book* (New York: Pinnacle Books, 1984), p. 102. For a version without any animal at all, see Blanche Knott, *Truly Tasteless Jokes* (New York: Ballantine Books, 1982), p. 46.

No one wants to be called or thought of as an "asshole." This is the basic import of the following greeting card parody collected in San Rafael, California, in December, 1989. The marked contrast between the intial religious sentiment and the final earthy put-down heightens the card's impact. The symbolic nuance of praying hands and a wreath provide additional support for the first impression of what promises to be a pious message. However, the circle formed by the wreath turns out to be holy in quite a different sense.

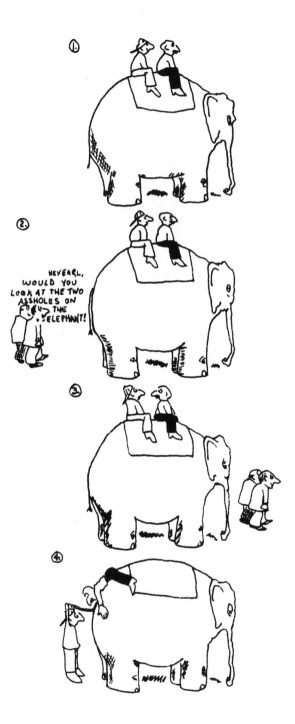

Never Try to Teach a Pig to Sing

Jesus Loves You

Everyone else thinks you're an asshole.

Never Try to Teach a Pig to Sing

179. One of Us Is an Asshole!

It is no more absurd for two birds to have one asshole than for one elephant to have two. The confusion between literal and metaphorical levels of understanding also provides the basis of humor in the following cartoon with its avian Siamese twins. It was collected from a nurse in a Seattle, Washington, doctor's office in 1983.

A second item, from Oakland, California, in March 1990, implies that there may be more than one "asshole" in an office or organization.

"One of us is an asshole!"

If Assholes Could Fly This Place Would Be An Airport

Never Try to Teach a Pig to Sing

180. Knock It Off Asshole!

    Sex between inappropriate partners is another theme found in folklore. Whether it is miscegenation, bestiality, or any form of so-called mixed marriage, the false sex object seems to be an ever popular subject of humor. In the following cartoon, which we have collected coast to coast—this version is from Berkeley in 1980—we have a French fried potato cut in a shape similar to that of a caterpillar, a French fry which can speak by the way. We have the victimized French fry protesting the sexual harassment by the aggressive caterpillar. Unwanted sex is an important element in the feminist critique of male deportment. For a version reported from England where French fries are better known as "chips," see RJ, 81.

181. Love's Labor Lost

The theme of mechanical sex is suggested in the cartoon presented below. Another theme is that of indiscriminate male sexuality, which is supposedly unleashed on the nearest convenient (sex) object. The fact that the object of lovemaking in the cartoon is a pull-toy suggests the masturbatory motion of "pulling one's pud." (Masturbation as a possible sexual outlet is not encouraged either in folklore or fact. See E. H. Hare, "Masturbatory Insanity: The History of an Idea," *Journal of Mental Science* 108 [1962], 1–25; and Robert H. MacDonald, "The Frightful Consequences of Onanism: Notes on the History of a Delusion," *Journal of the History of Ideas* 28 [1967], 423–31.) The title "Love's Labor Lost," perhaps borrowed from Shakespeare's early comedy of the same name, may reflect the Puritan view in which sexuality was sinful except for the express purpose of reproduction of the species.

The first version was collected in Oakland in 1975 on a piece of paper bearing an address in Charlotte, North Carolina, and a date of 1967. The second version is from ISR. A third text from Winnipeg in 1980 involves a dog and a car rather than a toy.

182. Guess Who?

In American folklore, there are a number of playful traditions in which one individual pretends to conceal his identity from a member of the opposite sex. Valentine's Day cards among others may be signed "Guess Who?" by someone who presumably is well known to the recipient. Similarly, at a party or even a chance meeting, a person might come up behind a friend, place his hands over the unsuspecting victim's eyes and say "Guess Who?"

In the following folk cartoon, this harmless teasing behavior has become a sexual act. The victim in the cartoon is perhaps expected to identify the unknown party on the basis of sexual features or performance. The cartoon may also represent a folk commentary on casual or anonymous sex or promiscuity in general.

The first version is from San Francisco and dates from the 1940s. The second was collected in Tennessee in 1977. (A version in which the victim is a French poodle appears as the frontispiece in J. M. Elgart, *More Over Sexteen* [New York: Grayson, 1953]). See also *Furthermore Over Sexteen*, Vol. 4 (New York: Grayson, 1956), p. 15.

Guess Who

GUESS WHO?

183. He Likes You

Some individuals who do not have dogs as beloved pets may feel victimized by the pets of neighbors. Dog owners in urban environments may be forced to walk their dogs with a leash, but they still allow their pets to urinate and defecate on public property and in other people's yards. Pets, like children, can be spoiled and undisciplined.

In the following cartoon, a dog owner shows little sympathy for his fellow human. After permitting his dog to greet the passerby effusively at the very least, his only comment is that the dog likes the put-upon man. Apparently, the cartoon is a critical commentary on excessive permissiveness.

We have some fifteen versions of this cartoon from coast to coast. We shall present only three. The earliest in our possession was collected in San Francisco in November 1973, and it bears the name of "Caldwell," who is a well-known American cartoonist. However, only five of our fifteen texts include his name. Assuming that he was indeed the originator of the cartoon some time before 1974 (and that he did not borrow it from folk tradition), we may have here an instance of a professionally drawn cartoon entering office copier tradition. We have a version from the fall of 1974 *without* Caldwell's name. The three texts shown below are from Chicago in 1983, Oakland in 1981, and New York City in 1981. Each version presents distinct differences in the cartoon characters, and these indicate that re-drawing has occured. Note the placement of the caption, the pants style, the dog markings (including teeth), the walkway, the shirt pocket of the victim, the face of the dog owner, the hairstyles of both the dog owner and the victim, etc.

"He likes you!"

Never Try to Teach a Pig to Sing

"He likes you"

Never Try to Teach a Pig to Sing

184. The Flasher

People as well as dogs can inflict sexual harassment on innocent bystanders. One form of sexual exhibitionism is called "flashing." It refers to an individual, usually male, who exposes his genitals in public to an unwilling audience. The stereotype of the flasher has him wearing a trench-coat and nothing else. To flash, he simply opens the coat. In the following folk cartoon sequence, the flasher literally gets his comeuppance. By flashing the occupants of an elevator, he truly has a captive audience that is unable to exit. However, the act of closing the elevator door and pushing the up button results in the flasher's being hoist on his own petard as Shakespeare put it in *Hamlet*, Act III, iv, 206. The closing of the elevator door would also appear to represent a form of symbolic castration. For an English version, see TCB, 121. This text was collected in Berkeley in 1982.

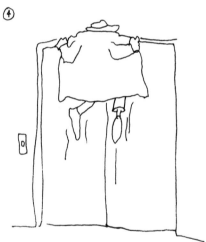

Never Try to Teach a Pig to Sing

185. Reproduction Is Fun

Among the animals featured in folklore, the rabbit is one of the most popular. One reason for this may be its primary association with fertility. Carrying a rabbit's foot (often on a key ring) for good luck may have phallic overtones. A popular European folktale, the "Rabbit-Herd" (Aarne-Thompson tale type 570), consists of a boy's keeping his (or a king's) rabbit(s) under control in order to win his bride, the king's daughter. In the tale, the king and his daughters try unsuccessfully to buy the hero's magic pipe or "seed drill"(!) with which he controls his rabbit charges. (For an unexpurgated version of the tale, see Vance Randolph, *Pissing in the Snow & Other Ozark Folktales* [Urbana: University of Illinois Press, 1976], pp. 47–49; cf. Legman, NLM, 179–80.) There is also a common folk idiom to "fuck like a bunny [rabbit]." Legman has surveyed some of the standard jokes treating rabbits and their reputation for rapid and prolific mating. One which he cited from California in 1941: "A male and female rabbit are hiding in a thicket from a pack of wolves: 'Shall we make a run for it, or outnumber them?' See RDJ, 193–94.

The first version of the following folk cartoon was collected at the Lawrence Radiation Lab, Livermore, California, in 1969. The second version was collected in Colorado in 1975. The motto could well serve for the entire paperwork empire insofar as the reproduction of xerographic folklore is fun. In fact, it is surely the inspiration for the title of *Reproduction Is Fun* (RIF). The cartoon also appears as the frontispiece in one of the Colorado collections of photocopier folklore. Cf. UFFC-TB, ii; for four other versions, see UFFC-PC, 120–23.

Never Try to Teach a Pig to Sing

REPRODUCTION

IS FUN

186. Escargot

In contrast to rabbits who move quickly, snails are known for moving very slowly. In the following cartoon, the snail's role as a culinary delicacy, especially in France, is featured. The French term for snails is escargot. However, eating escargot becomes more than a gourmet treat in the context of the cartoon. It must also be remembered that part of the stereotype of the French lover includes an alleged association with oral sex.

A text from Indianapolis in 1976 (not presented here) bears an attribution to "Leggett," but none of our other texts, including the two which follow, contain any authorial ascription at all. The first version was collected from a Toyota garage in Berkeley in 1982, while the second was also found in Berkeley in 1985.

WHERE DID YOU EVER LEARN TO EAT ESCARGOT LIKE THAT?

WHERE DID YOU LEARN TO EAT
ESCARGOT LIKE THAT?

The Battle of the Sexes

Tensions between men and women are presumably as old as humankind itself. There is no society on earth which does not specify the division of labor by sex. Men's roles and women's roles are usually delineated in each society, and they are typically distinct from one another. It may also be true that to some extent each gender envies the other.

In the twentieth century, the rise of feminism and women's rights groups (finally gaining women's suffrage in the United States in 1920 with the ratification of the nineteenth amendment to the Constitution) has moved women closer to equality with men, especially in the economic and political arenas. Women's gains, however, have not always come easily or without resistance from old-fashioned conservative males. In this context, women's advances toward theoretical parity with men have, if anything, created increased tension between the sexes. Competition between women and men is now to be found in nearly all areas of activity, at least in the United States and Western Europe.

It should come as no surprise to learn that modern photocopier folklore richly reflects the revolutionary changes that have taken place in the struggle to obtain women's rights. Some of the materials celebrate the newly won opportunities; some of the materials articulate the anxiety felt by males in the wake of women's successes. We feel that the photocopier folklore deriving from the contemporary battle of the sexes in the United States is of sufficient significance to warrant concluding this volume with representative examples. In this concluding chapter, we have abandoned our usual generic constraints in favor of thematic unity. Thus, we shall present cartoons, jokes, wallet cards, notices, and folk poetry, all of which we believe to be germane to the depiction of the never-ending battle of the sexes.

187. The Evolution of Authority

An important part of the power struggle between men and women concerns who is in command. Do women follow men's orders? Or do men follow women's orders? In individual households, a wife or a husband may be the dominant decision maker.

In the following folk cartoon sequence, a hypothetical scheme of evolution is postulated. By means of mere footprints, the viewer can readily see that the first stage of the development of power belonged to a pre-human ancestor. This was followed by a naked footprint, presumably representing so-called primitive man. The third phase was dominated by modern males as symbolized by the outline of a male shoe. But according to the schema, the final stage is controlled by women as signaled by the imprint of a high heel of a woman's shoe. The invoking of the term "evolution" also implies that men are more primitive than women or to put it another way, women are a higher form of life than men. It should be noted that all of our exemplars, including the two presented here, were collected from women. The first version was collected from a female executive secretary working for an investment firm in Ross, California, in 1986, while the second was collected in a women's dormitory room at the University of California, Berkeley, in 1987. The two versions also serve to demonstrate once again the nature of variation in folklore. Even a fairly simple design has obviously been re-drawn rather than just reproduced.

THE EVOLUTION OF AUTHORITY

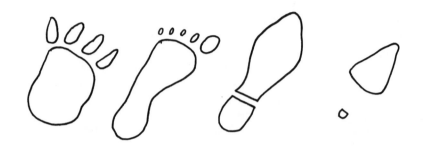

The evolution of authority.

Never Try to Teach a Pig to Sing

188. Why Not a "Male" Boat?

The following item, collected from the Bethel Island Marina in northern California in 1977 from a male boat owner, purports to explain the venerable nautical tradition of referring to a ship or boat as "She." This extended double entendre articulates a male view of women. For a Swedish version, see MF, 81.

Why not a "Male" boat?

A boat is called a "She" because:
- *there's always a gang of men around*
- *she has a waist and stays*
- *she takes a lot of paint to keep her looking good*
- *it's not the initial expense that breaks you, its the upkeep*

- *it takes a good man to handle her right*
- *she shows her topsides, hides her bottom and when coming into port always heads for the buoys*

189. Diary of a Young Lady

The male stereotype of women is also reflected in the following item from a female secretary in a law firm in San Francisco. She had been collecting office-copier folklore for nearly sixty years. She died in 1975. The item, a wallet card, was not dated, but it apparently goes back to the days when trans-Atlantic ocean voyages were in vogue, that is, prior to World War II.

DIARY OF A YOUNG LADY CROSSING
THE OCEAN FOR THE FIRST TIME

Monday—I feel highly honored for being placed at the Captain's table.

Tuesday—I spent the morning on the bridge with the Captain. He seems to like me.

Wednesday—The Captain made proposals to me unbecoming an officer and a gentleman.

Thursday—The Captain threatened to sink the ship unless I agreed to his proposals.

Friday—I saved six hundred lives.

190. How to Tell a Businessman from a Businesswoman

The increasing concern in American society with the rights of women has drawn attention to the dangers of stereotyping. A woman competing in a "man's world" has a terrible dilemma. If she acts out the passive role traditionally expected (by males), then she runs the risk of being judged less competent than more active employees. If, on the other hand, she assumes an active role, she runs the risk of being considered too aggressive and she may again fail to succeed.

The above no-win situation, of course, is applicable to some extent to all employees, male and female. The nuances of proper behavior can be subtle indeed. Thrifty is admirable but stingy is not. The line is sometimes hard to draw and not everyone would agree on where the line is or should be drawn.

In the first example, collected in Oakland in 1977, women are depicted as being penalized for the same behavior for which men are rewarded. In another version (not presented here), collected from a female manager of a clothing store in Indianapolis in 1976, most of the comparisons are the same. However, variations include the businesswoman being "stubborn" rather than "hard," and "opinionated" rather than "mouthy," while the businessman is "discreet" rather than "close-mouthed." For another version, see YD [125].

In a second item in which male and female behavior is contrasted, a similar misogynist viewpoint is manifested. Although the two items are not related, it is interesting to see the thematic overlap. For example, both items end with a male stereotypic reference to menstruation. The item was collected in Tennessee in March 1990 and is similar to versions circulating in California.

HOW TO TELL A BUSINESSMAN FROM A BUSINESSWOMAN

A businessman—	A businesswoman—
is aggressive	is pushy
is good on details	is picky
follows through	doesn't know when to quit
stands firm	is hard
is a man of the world	has been around
is not afraid to say what he thinks	is mouthy
exercises authority diligently	is power-mad
is close-mouthed	is secretive
is a stern taskmaster	is hard to work for
drinks because of the excessive job pressure	is a lush
loses his temper because he is so involved in his job	is bitchy
when he's depressed (hungover), everyone tiptoes past his office	when she is moody, it must be "her time of the month".

The Rules

1.)The *Female Always* Makes The Rules.
2.)The Rules are Subject to Change at any Time *without prior Notification*
3.)*No Male* can Possibly Know all the Rules
4.)If the *Female* Suspects the *Male* Knows all the Rules, she must Immediately change some or all of the Rules
5.)The *Female* is NEVER wrong
6.)If the *Female* is WRONG, it is because of a Flagrant Misunderstanding which was a Direct Result of something the *Male* did or said wrong
7.)If the Rule 6 applies, the *Male* must Apologize Immediately for causing the Misunderstanding
8.)The *Female* can change her mind at any given point in time
9.)The *Male* must NEVER change his mind without Express Written Consent from the *Female*
10.)The *Female* has every right to be Angry or Upset *at any time*
11.)The *Male* must remain Calm at ALL Times, unless the *Female* wants him to be angry or upset
12.)The *Female* must Under NO Circumstances let the *Male* know whether or not she wants him to be angry or upset
13.)*Any Attempt to Document these Rules could result in Bodily Harm*
14.)If the *Female* has PMS, *All Rules are Null and Void*

Never Try to Teach a Pig to Sing

191. Boys!!

Women's difficulties start much earlier than their entry into the business world. Even as adolescent girls, they are faced with critical choices as to how to behave toward members of the opposite sex. In the following item collected from a female informant in Washington, D.C., in 1976, the alternatives for teenage girls are spelled out. Once again, it appears to be a no-win situation. Whatever a girl does, she risks criticism and rejection.

Boys !!

If you smile at him, he thinks you're flirting
If you don't, he thinks you're stuck up.
If you let him kiss you, he wishes you were more
reserved.

If you don't, he thinks you're an iceburg
If you flatter him, he thinks you're simple
If you don't, he thinks you don't understand
him.

If you tell him you love him he thinks you're
proposing
If you don't, he thinks you don't care
If you are a good girl, you aren't human
If you return his caress, he doesn't want you
If you let him make love to you, you're
cheap
If you don't, he'll go out with a girl that
will.

If you go out with other boys, he thinks
you're fickle.

If you don't, he thinks no one will have
you.

Boys!!! God bless 'em, they don't know what
they want.

192. I Don't Drink

In the following text apparently written from a girl's perspective, she does seem to know her own mind with respect to how to treat boys. The text, collected in San Francisco in 1964, is an example of a wallet card passed out by girls. The content is somewhat similar to an oral chant, "I don't smoke and I don't chew and I don't go with boys who do," which was popular at Miami High School in 1950. In the present text, note the possible double meaning of the last line.

> I don't drink
> I don't smoke
> I don't make out with boys
>
> What do I do for fun?
> I lie

193. The Silent Salesman

A more elaborate type of a date card consists of a direct request for sexual intercourse. The first version was collected in Tennessee in 1977. The second version presented here was handed to a middle-aged female in the Imperial Hotel in Tokyo, in 1967, by the captain of an American passenger liner. Fortunately for us, she kept the card! Versions of this card in ISR collected from Nevada and California in the early 1960s bear such titles as "I am a Silent Salesman" and "The Silent Bartender." (For another version, entitled "I'm the Silent Type," see UFFC-TB, v.) The third version circulated in 1975 in one of the administrative offices of the Department of anthropology at the University of California, Berkeley. It actually functions as a type of catch inasmuch as the card is made of strong plastic which cannot be torn.

YOU APPEAL TO ME.

I WOULD LIKE TO SLEEP WITH YOU

IF INTERESTED KEEP THIS CARD.

IF NOT INTERESTED RETURN CARD PLEASE.

(I'M RUNNING OUT OF CARDS)

Any chance to crawl in the sack with
you tonight?
If so, keep this card. If not, kindly
return, as they are expensive.
I am not as good as I once was,
BUT I am as good ONCE as I ever was.

P.S. You don't have to say yes. JUST SMILE!

If You're In The Mood For Sex

KEEP THIS CARD & SMILE

If You're Not In The Mood

TEAR THIS CARD UP

194. I'm Kind of the "Shy Type"

An alternative date card feigns shyness before concluding with the same old request. This card is reminiscent of a traditional joke in which a not-too-bright young man tries to follow the advice of a suave older friend who urges him to discuss books or theater before making sexual advances. See RDJ, 223. The card was collected in San Francisco in 1977. (For another version, see UFFC-TB, v.)

HI

I'M KIND OF THE "SHY TYPE" AND THIS IS REALLY EMBARRASSING FOR ME.

WOULD IT BE TOO FORWARD OF ME TO INVITE YOU OVER FOR A KIND OF "GET ACQUAINTED" COCKTAIL?

IT WOULD BE JUST SWELL TALKING TO YOU ABOUT WHERE YOU ARE FROM. AND DISCUSSING THE WEATHER AND EVERYTHING. THEN WE COULD FUCK.

195. Notice Me Dammit!!

Salesmen are constantly looking for ways to attract attention from prospective clients. Sexuality constitutes a large portion of commercial advertising, but to a sated or jaded public, such techniques may be ignored. The following cartoon sequences make fun of the efforts to which some salesmen might go to arouse the interest of clients. A possible larger theme might be the cry of an individual for attention in a complex, populous society which pays no mind to the ordinary. It is only the extraordinary, the sensational, which causes other individuals to take notice, a condition which seems to permeate American media such as radio, television, and newspapers.

In this version collected in Kokomo in 1976, the female protagonist cries in despair at her failure to interest a blasé male bar patron. (The equation of hooker with salesman also suggests that the latter must often prostitute themselves in order to be successful. See "Every Day of My Life, item 175 above.)

Never Try to Teach a Pig to Sing

196. So What's So Great?

Taboo activities are frequently referred to by means of conventional euphemistic circumlocutions. This is especially the case when speaking to children about such activities. In the following cartoon, we find a child's misunderstanding of the phrase "to sleep together." The cartoon, collected in San Francisco in 1978 but dating back to 1955, employs characters from the well-known "Peanuts" comic strip created by Charles M. Schulz. For two other versions, see UFFC-PC, 36–37; for English versions, see TCB, 11 and RJ, 114.

So Whats So Great About Sleeping Together?

197. O.K.! We Took Off Our Clothes . . .

Children's supposed misunderstanding of adult sexuality is also the theme of the following cartoon collected in Ripon, California, in 1988. Part of the humor comes from the standard dialogue of the battle of the sexes being placed in the mouths of young children. Even the conventional "headache" excuse offered by women to avoid unwanted sexual activity—it is a code to be used rather than a direct refusal—is found in the cartoon. In this case, the young girl would certainly seem to have a legitimate reason to have a headache. One is also tempted to speculate that the position of the boy standing on the head of the girl, like the so-called "normal" position for heterosexual coitus, is a not-so-subtle metaphor for male domination in American culture: men on top, women on the bottom. For another version, see RJ, 115.

198. The Pacifier

Pacifiers are commonly used in infant care to keep babies happy or at least to stop them from crying. It is not always entirely clear whether they are for the infant's benefit or for the infant's parents' welfare. In the following folk cartoon collected from a female informant who worked as a bank teller in Hayward, California, we see the pacifier employed differently for the female baby than for the male. The scene is notable for its overt reference to masturbatory activity and to the explicit recognition of female pleasure in sexuality. These themes were rarely articulated prior to the advent of the feminist movement. For a German text, see IK, 94.

199. Well! What Are You Staring At?

The awareness of sexual anatomical differences is a source of curiosity among both sexes. From early childhood on, each sex is fascinated by the genitalia of the other, and how they operate, for example, with respect to urination.

In the following folk cartoon which dates from the World War II era, a man and a woman in the Navy are shown at a men's urinal. The scene is total fantasy because any male military bathroom facility would normally include a sit-down toilet. During World War II, women were asked to take the place of men in factories and to some extent in the military. No doubt this caused some concern on the part of males. How could women use the "facilities"? This is the subject of the cartoon presented below. The first version was collected in San Francisco during World War II; the second from the Coast Guard ship U.S.S. *Richardson* circa 1945.

"WELL! WHAT ARE YOU STARING AT?"

"Well What The Hell Are You Looking At"

200. There *Is* a Difference

Sex differences are a fact of life. This is so regardless of the issue of equality of the sexes before the law. Young children usually discover the differences in external genital features between males and females relatively early by observing either parents or siblings in the nude. The French phrase "Vive la différence!" which expresses gratitude for the differences (because they lead to mutually pleasurable sexual interaction), may not apply to the reactions of young children who tend rather to be initially curious and uneasy about the comparison of male and female sexual characteristics.

The first version of the following cartoon was collected in 1974 from the Naval Air Station in Alameda, California. The caption, supposedly contrasting Naval aviators from sailors, in some versions simply states, "There is a difference." The cartoon goes back at least to the years of World War II. The second version, collected from a female informant in Wheaton, Maryland, in 1981, reflects a more modern feminist perspective concerned with the unfair salary differential between male and female employees of the same firm.

For other versions entitled "Vive la différence," see *Still More Over Sexteen* (Secaucus, New Jersey: Castle Books, 1973), p. 9; RIF, 4. For another version, see YD [111]. For a Danish version, see CS, 89; for a German version, see IK, 21. For an English parallel to the second text, see RIF, 141.

There is a difference
between Aviators
and other Sailors

oh, that explains the difference
in our salaries!

201. No You Can't Touch It

In this interesting cartoon collected from a Wave at the Naval Air Station in Alameda, California, in 1975, we find several important psychological themes. First, there is the idea that females once had penises, but they lost them. Second, there is the male's fear that if a female touches his organ, it will be destroyed. The fear of a castrating woman is very much a part of American folklore (and the folklore of many other cultures as well). Legman (RDJ, 526, cf. also 117) refers to a version of this image (though with no reference to a cartoon) from New York City in 1948. For another version (without a cartoon), see Shelli Sonstein, *The Thoroughly Tasteful Dirty Joke Book* (New York: Stein and Day, 1985), p. 122. For an English version, see TCB, 120.

NO YOU CAN'T TOUCH IT,
YOU'VE BROKEN YOURS OFF ALREADY

202. So Hot It Melted

Male impotence is a recurring theme in humor. There may be anxiety about impotence before the act and if impotence should occur, the male may feel great embarrassment and compelled to offer some kind of excuse or explanation no matter how feeble or far-fetched. Female frigidity is not as obvious as male impotence. In the following folk cartoon from Sacramento in 1978, a male offers a rather fanciful rationale for his predicament.

"I think it got so hot it melted"

203. I've Got Six Marbles

In American culture, the rise of women's liberation has surely encouraged women to challenge the boasting, aggressive male. In the following very popular folk cartoon, the debate eventually comes down to comparative anatomy. Penis envy is dismissed with the female indicating her avowed intention to use her sexuality to control males and get ahead.

The first version was collected in Kokomo in 1976. We are reproducing this version just as it is. Clearly cutting off the bottom of the page represents a form of censorship to avoid an explicit display of sexual parts. The second version was collected in Berkeley in 1985, and it represents an uncut version of the cartoon sequence. (Two versions similar to the two presented here are contained in UFFC-PC, 50–51, except that interestingly enough, it is the analog to our first version which is not cut off and the analog to our second which is. This confirms the traditionality of intentionally cutting off the lower portions of the bottom series.) For a version (without the cartoon drawings), see Mr. "J," *Still More of the World's Best Dirty Jokes* (Secaucus, New Jersey: Castle, 1981), p. 97. For a Danish version, see CS, 59.

Never Try to Teach a Pig to Sing

204. So That's Why

As suggested by the preceding example, sexual curiosity and exploration are a normal part of the childhood experience. According to Freudian theory, little girls upon discovering that little boys possess penises interpret this as an anatomical lack in themselves. Too much emphasis may have been placed upon what psychoanalysts have termed penis envy—it turns out that males also envy females, especially their biological ability to bear children. But it would appear that penis envy on the part of females and pregnancy envy on the part of males might just be a part of general pan-human psychology. In any case, with respect to American culture, we can see in the following cartoons collected in San Francisco in 1976, Sacramento in 1979, and Eureka in 1989 an explicit articulation of penis envy. Among the many versions of this item we have seen, we have noted differences in the facial expression. In most, he is frowning, but in a few he is smiling. The fact that the masculine attributes are described in automotive terms is surely related to the tendency among some American adolescent boys to exhibit their machismo by "souping up" their "hot rods." For a version (without the cartoon), see Blanche Knott, *Truly Tasteless Jokes IV* (New York: Pinnacle Books, 1984), p. 64. For an English version, see RIF, 83.

So THAT'S why LiTTLE
boys can run FASter
Than little girls ---
BALL BEARINGS !!!
(and a stick shift)

"So that's why Little
Boys can run faster
than little girls .....
Ball-Bearings and a
Stick shift too !! "

SO THAT'S WHY LITTLE
BOYS CAN RUN FASTER
THAN LITTLE GIRLS....
"BALL BEARINGS!!!"
(AND A STICK SHIFT!)

205. How Do I Know What She Wants?

Lessons learned when young about sexual differences carry over into adult life. In the following folk cartoon, there are several additional themes. First of all, there is the matter of the relationship between the sexes in a military occupation zone. Women in wartime may be forced to earn their living through fraternization with the victorious soldiers. A second theme is the sexually innocent if not ignorant American soldier who seemingly fails to understand the overtures of a native woman. In view of the historical American military involvement in Japan, Korea, and Viet Nam, it is not at all surprising that the setting in most versions of this cartoon is Asian. The first version was collected in Winnipeg in 1980 while the second was collected in Los Angeles in 1989. For a German version, see IK, 100.

"How do I know what she wants?...
She can't speak a word of English!"

"HOW DO I KNOW WHAT SHE
WANTS? SHE CAN'T SPEAK
A WORD OF ENGLISH!"

206. Now That's Italian

A similar fondling image is found in an Italian restaurant setting. Here the seductive waitress with a short dress (perhaps required by the male management) makes a passing gesture. The phrase "Now that's Italian" may be a play on an American commercial advertisement for a salad dressing or a tomato sauce. This would explain why the double entendre requires the man to be an Italian chef tasting his latest culinary creation. The cartoon was collected in Winnipeg in 1980.

"Now that's Italian"

207. Hi. Gotcha!

Sometimes grabbing the genitals can be playful and affectionate, but sometimes it may be an aggressive and painful attack. In the following folk cartoon collected in the Richmond, California, Police Department, in 1983, but evidently set in Dade County, Florida, a woman successfully grabs the genitals of a surprised male in an adjoining bathroom. The phrase "Gotcha" connotes catching someone off guard.

An older parallel theme involves a goose attacking a Black boy through a fence. In the context of the folklore of race relations in the United States, one must keep in mind the white stereotypic image of the super-phallic Black male. The fear of such males by whites surely was a factor in the perpetration of mob lynchings and, more to the point, castrations. The second cartoon presented below circulated in the early 1940s (and probably earlier). It depicts a fantasized rendering of this castration impulse. The caption on the third exemplar expresses an unequivocal racist commentary in favor of segregation. It was collected in 1947 in New York City but clearly refers to Tampa, Florida. For an additional version—with a white boy—see *Over Sexteen* (New York: Elgart, 1951), p. 27. Cf. RJ, 63.

DADE COUNTY COURTHOUSE REST ROOMS

Never Try to Teach a Pig to Sing

208. Let's Hear It Meow!

One of the common slang terms for vagina is "pussy" (cf. item 120 above). The term appears in countless jokes. For example, in one, an elementary school teacher informs her new class that her name is Miss Prussy, "that's pussy with an 'r.'" The next day when she asks if anyone remembers her name, a little boy raises his hand and says that he does. "It's Miss Crunt!" Related idioms include "pussywhipped," which refers pejoratively to a male dominated by a female.

In the first cartoon below, collected in Tennessee in 1977, knowledge of the meaning of "pussy" is assumed. Perhaps the reason for the association of pussy with pudendum is the analogy between fur and hair. In this instance, there is at least a suggestion that the boy is somewhat fearful of the pussy. If it is to meow, then it must have a mouth. The image of the vagina as mouth may well evoke the castration anxiety caused by the traditional notion of the *vagina dentata*, a motif with virtual worldwide distribution. It is probably too far fetched to attach any significance to the spelling "meow" instead of "miaow" or "miaou" for the mewing sound of the cat. "Me ow" in such a context might otherwise constitute a succinct two-word summation of the boy's fear of the female genitalia. A second version from Eureka, California, in late 1989, attests to the national dispersion of the item as well as demonstrating variation, especially in the drawing.

The third cartoon, collected in Oakland in 1980, also plays upon the same term. In this case, there is an additional double entendre referring both to a drunk cat and a small vagina, the latter deemed desirable by males. We should note too that once again we have a fine example of a cartoon based upon the literalization of a metaphor. For an English version of the second cartoon, see RIF, 74.

IF IT REALLY IS ONE, LET ME HEAR IT 'MEOW'!

happiness is a tight pussy

209. Love Is . . .

In addition to the many "Peanuts" parodies, there are many other popular cartoon characters which serve as inspiration for folk artists. We have already seen Donald Duck and Mickey Mouse. One such series by syndicated cartoonist Kim Casali has to do with an innocent couple illustrating a series of pseudo-proverbial, frequently saccharine captions invariably beginning with "Love is . . .".

The following folk cartoon collected at Providence Hospital in Oakland in 1977 transforms an innocuous platitude into an explicit double entendre. A second version from Iselin, New Jersey, in 1984 has a different caption taken from the American Telephone and Telegraph advertising commercial of the 1980s. The same commercial line, incidentally, is utilized in a cross-breed riddle: "What do you get when you cross a rooster and a telephone pole?" Answer: "A forty foot cock that wants to reach out and touch someone." For a German text of the cartoon, see IK, 105.

Never Try to Teach a Pig to Sing

The Bell System

.... REACH OUT...
REACH OUT AND TOUCH SOMEONE

210. Let's Play Pregnant

A popular way of ventilating anxieties about sex differences is to project adult sex roles upon young children, as we have already demonstrated. Of course, children are genuinely concerned with such matters, and they are particularly affected by the observation of pregnancy. Whether it is the fear of being displaced by a younger sibling rival or whether it is worry caused by the sight of a newly expectant mother undergoing the throes of morning sickness, children do frequently act out in fantasy form various kinds of adult behavior.

In the following example, collected in Kokomo in 1976, we find the implicit disparity between male and female roles in childbearing at issue. The contrast between a man's shaving (which is not all that difficult or painful) and a woman's suffering nausea is obvious. It is very likely the male's deep feeling of inequality with respect to producing children has led to the custom of couvade which is nearly worldwide in distribution. In couvade (from the French "couver" to hatch), it is the man who observes dietary taboos or goes to bed in order to facilitate childbirth either before or during his wife's actual parturition period. Legman (NLM, 402; cf. RDF, 687) reports a similar caption (but with no reference to a cartoon) from New York City in 1952: Little Boy: "Let's play house." Little Girl: "All right. You shave and I'll vomit." For another version, see *More Over Sexteen* (New York: Grayson, 1953), p. 30.

"Let's play pregnant. I'll shave and you'll throw up."

Never Try to Teach a Pig to Sing

211. It Aint' Easy Being a Dick

Quite a bit of imagination is displayed in anthropomorphizing a phallus and testicles. A clever series of puns playing upon sexual metaphors covers a range of topics, including friends, neighbors, and masturbation. The perception of the end of the urethra as an eye is well established in numerous jokes and in all probability it is related to the evil eye tradition. (See Alan Dundes, *Interpreting Folklore* [Bloomington: Indiana University Press, 1980], pp. 115–19, for a detailed discussion of the folk notion of the penis as one-eyed.)

Parts of the verbal text in the following item are reminiscent of traditional riddles, e.g., "What has a head and can't think? A match." "What has eyes and cannot see? A potato." One can even cite a partial parallel text in the form of a riddle: "What's the dumbest part of a man? His prick. It's got no brains, its best friends are two nuts, and it lives next door to an asshole." See Blanche Knott, *Truly Tasteless Jokes Two* (New York: Ballantine Books, 1983), p. 50. The text presented here was collected from a female secretary in Fremont, California, in 1987.

Never Try to Teach a Pig to Sing

212. Two Old Duffle Bags

Another metaphorical mode of referring to a phallus involves military terminology. Recruits at boot camp used to be taught "This is my rifle; this is my gun; this is for killing; this is for fun." The gun as opposed to the rifle was the phallus.

In the following joke collected in Foster City, California, in 1986, the man offers one metaphor but his secretary retorts with another. The use of euphemisms in this battle of the sexes is common. Other standard circumlocutions for an open trousers' fly include "Your barndoor is open" and "It's one o'clock in the button factory." For a variant text in which it is a garage door which is open, revealing a "little pink Volkswagen with two flat tires up front," see *Playboy's Party Jokes 6* (New York: PBJ Books, 1974), p. 132.

Mr. Smith got himself a new secretary. She was young, sweet and polite. One day while taking dictation, she noticed his fly was open and on leaving the room; she said, "Oh, Mr. Smith, did you know that your barracks door is open?"

He did not understand her remark, but later on he happened to look down and saw that his zipper was open. He decided to have some fun with his secretary. Calling her in, he asked, "By the way, Miss Jones, when you saw my barracks door open this morning did you also see a soldier standing at attention?"

She was quite witty. "Why no, Mr. Smith," she replied. "All I saw was a disabled veteran sitting on two old duffle bags?"

213. Let the Following Story Be a Warning to You

The fable form may involve human characters as well as animal. What is typical of the fable genre is that some kind of moral or message is intended to be communicated by the narrative. Often the fable genre overlaps with the exemplum tradition in which narratives are specifically employed as "examples" of normative behavior. Ministers frequently use exempla in their weekly sermons to emphasize a particular point.

The very title of the first version of the following text collected in Long Beach, California, in 1975, suggests that an exemplum will be presented. In this case, the parody includes advertising commercials, especially those in which one housewife questions another as to how she manages to achieve such feats as the whiteness of her sheets, the sweetness of her breath, or the spotlessness of her dishes. Judging from the variety of such commercials, there seem to be no restrictions as to the degree of neighborly curiosity about the state of a friend's dentures, personal hygiene, or toilet bowl.

In the first version, the taking of a housewife's advice leads to disaster. Besides castration, there may also be a reference to the law requiring cigarette packages to be labeled with the warning that smoking may be hazardous to one's health, a reference which is made explicit in the subtitle of the second version collected in Washington, D.C., in 1977. The second version differs markedly from the first with respect to the basic premise, the title, the inclusion of an illustrative cartoon, and the absence of any allusion to castration, among other details. Yet surely both versions belong to a common folkloristic tradition. Legman reports a version from New York City dating from 1951. See NLM, 443, cf. 972. Also see J. M. Elgart, *More Over Sexteen* (New York: Grayson, 1953), p. 112, and Julius Alvin, *Utterly Gross Jokes*, Vol. III (New York: Zebra Books, 1984), p. 128.

Strangely enough, this item surfaced in August 1988, purporting to be a true story. It was reported first in the *Jerusalem Post*, and then it was picked up by Reuters. It was broadcast on National Public Radio as an authentic news event. In this version, an Israeli housewife, unable to kill a cockroach, threw it into a toilet and sprayed insecticide on it. Later her husband dropped a cigarette butt into the toilet bowl. This ignited the fumes and seriously burned his "sensitive parts." When the medical team arrived at the house and heard the details, they laughed so hard that they dropped the stretcher down the stairs, breaking the man's pelvis.

When challenged about the story's authenticity, the *Jerusalem Post* initially insisted that the incident was true and that the name of the man in question could not be released because sources requested medical secrecy. Eventually, however, the *Post* was forced to retract the story, admitting that one of its reporters had heard the story second-hand from an insurance agent and had failed to verify it. For details, see the *San Francisco Chronicle*, August 30, 1988, p. A13, "Cockroach Story Refuses to Die" and *San Francisco Chronicle*, September 1, 1988, "Cockroach Story Finally Dies." This incident would tend to make one consider the story a legend as well as a photocopier tradition. For legendary accounts of the "exploding toilet," see Paul Smith, *The Book of Nasty Legends* (London: Routledge & Kegan Paul, 1983), p. 48, and especially Jan Harold Brunvand, *The Mexican Pet: More "New" Urban Legends and Some Old Favorites* (New York: W. W. Norton, 1986), pp. 13–16.

GROUND ACCIDENT OF THE MONTH

OR

Smoking May Be Hazardous To Your Health

Recently, a man suffered injuries that required hospital attention - injuries
resulting from a bizarre accident, weird enough to satisfy Ripley himself.
It seems the accident resulted from a simple nuisance - a clogged
nozzle on a pressurized can of hair spray. The victim's wife had dumped a
substantial amount of the hair spray (containing alcohol) into the toilet in an
attempt to free the nozzle orifice with a safety pin. Leaving the commode
unflushed, she left the bathroom to her unsuspecting hubby. The husband
retired to the bathroom for his morning constitutional, sat down, lit a
cigarette, and dropped the match into the bowl. The resulting explosion
imbedded pieces of the toilet lid into the bathroom walls . . . and the victim's
posterior. It seems you're not safe anywhere any more.

Never Try to Teach a Pig to Sing

214. The New Gillette Stainless Steel Spoiler Blade

One thing which does give aggressive males pause is the fear of castration at the hand of or rather the genitals of a female sex object. The *vagina dentata* motif is one of the most widespread in the world (cf. Motif F 547.1.1, Vagina Dentata, in Stith Thompson, *Motif-Index of Folk-Literature*, 6 vols. [Bloomington: Indiana University Press, 1955–58]; and Legman, NLM, 427–74).

In the present text, it is a razor blade which serves the purpose. To the extent that hair is a sexual characteristic if not symbol, it is of interest that a razor blade should represent a castrating instrument. With this logic, the daily act of shaving could be construed as a symbolic self-castratory act. The tonsured head of the celibate priest as well as the supposed sexual innocence of "clean cut" young men are part of the same social symbolic code. Consider also that a "hairy" chest and facial hair (especially a mustache in Near Eastern cultures) are generally associated with masculinity. Thus, to cut one's hair is to diminish symbolically one's visible badge of sexuality—just as Samson's shorn locks signified his loss of virility and strength (Judges 16). For an extended discussion of the symbolism of hair, see Edmund R. Leach, "Magical Hair," *Journal of the Royal Anthropological Institute* 88 (1958), 147–64, and Gananath Obeyesekere, *Medusa's Hair: An Essay on Personal Symbols and Religious Experience* (Chicago: University of Chicago Press, 1981).

In the version of this text collected from San Francisco in 1977 as well as the version collected in Berkeley in the 1980s, the secret promiscuity of a woman is revealed showing the direst of consequences for her male companions. For a variant text reported from Fort Lauderdale, Florida, in 1953, see NLM, 448.

THE NEW GILLETTE STAINLESS
STEEL SPOILER BLADE

A lady swallowed a New Gillette Stainless Steel Blade and her family doctor discovered that not only had she given herself a tonsilectomy, appendectomy, and a hysterectomy, but had also castrated her husband, circumcised her neighbor, taken two fingers from a casual acquaintance, given her lover a hair-lip and there were still five shaves left.

The following is a sample of the new adult commercial that will be shown on t.v. this fall for the new Gillette SuperSpoiler blade—the S.S.

A nice lady accidently swallowed one of the new Gillette S.S. blades.

She was experiencing some discomfort and her doctor had discovered that in a week's time she not only had given herself a tonsilectomy, an appendectomy, and a complete hysterectomy, but she had already castrated her husband, circumcized her lover, and taken off the fingers of a casual acquaintance she had met at a cocktail party.

She had given her minister a hairlip and cut the top off her boss's tongue. But the most wonderful thing that the Gillette company discovered was that there were still twelve good shaves left in the blade.

215. The 747 Has Everything

A similar theme of castration is found in the following joke—also reported in oral tradition. In this case, the male victim is not quite so innocent inasmuch as he fails to follow instructions. The text is a popular one and was collected in xerographic form from coast to coast.

The version presented here was collected in Oakland in 1983. We noted earlier that it was difficult for a woman to use a man's urinal (item 199 above). In this text, it is the man who encounters problems when he uses a woman's bathroom—although the problems are fiction, not fact. In the context of the battle of the sexes, it is noteworthy that it is a female stewardess who initially warns the man how to behave and a female nurse who makes the final statement.

For other versions, see NLM, 658; Julius Alvin, *Gross Jokes* (New York: Zebra Books, 1983), p. 133; and Blanche Knott, *Truly Tasteless Jokes 3* (New York: Ballantine Books, 1983), p. 50. For an English version, see TCB, 157.

THE 747 HAS EVERYTHING

A man traveling by plane was in urgent need of using the men's room.

Each time he tried the door, it was occupied.

The stewardess, aware of his predicament, suggested that he use the ladies' room, but cautioned him against pressing any of the buttons on the wall. The buttons were marked "WW", "WA", "PP", and "ATR".

While sitting there, his curiosity eventually got the better of him.

He carefully pressed the first button marked "WW".

Immediately warm water sprayed over his entire ass.

He thought, "Golly, the gals really have it made."

Still curious, he pressed the button marked "WA".

Warm air dried his ass completely.

He thought, "This was just out of this world," when the third button marked "PP" yielded a large powder puff which powdered his bottom lightly with powder.

Naturally, he just couldn't resist the last one marked "ATR."

When he woke up in the hospital he panicked and rang for the nurse. "What happened?" he asked her. "The last thing I remember I was in the ladies' room aboard a plane."

The nurse replied, "Yes, you were having a great time until you pressed the button marked "ATR" which stands for "Automatic Tampax Remover".

"Your penis is under your pillow."

216. Women's Power

If women felt they could acquire power by castrating men, then a most appropriate symbol of such acquired power might very well be the following cartoon collected in Oakland in 1980.

217. I Assume

A prime arena for the battle of the sexes is the home front. While the home is often considered to be the woman's domain, she does on occasion request help with certain chores from the man of the house. Some men are handy with domestic tasks; some may shirk what they consider onerous jobs, but some utterly refuse to accept any responsibility for the daily maintenance and operation of the household.

One stereotype of the latter is the pot-bellied, middle-aged, beer-guzzling slob or "couch potato," an individual who seems to grow roots in the couch from watching countless hours of television, especially sporting events such as boxing, wrestling, football, etc. Such males may be the breadwinners, but in the home, they do little more than issue commands to their long-suffering wives.

Christmas represents a time of the year when wives may request some cooperation from their husbands. They may ask for help in buying a tree, decorating it, and setting up indoor or outdoor lights and displays. Although many families insist upon being reunited at home for Christmas, it can nevertheless be a time of considerable distress and tension. One reason for this is that Christmas in the United States is primarily a holiday for children—with Santa Claus bringing a bounty of presents. When children grow up, they discover as parents that Christmas is a lot of work and that one does far more giving than receiving. The disparity between the nostalgic remembrance of joyful children's Christmas celebrations in the past with the harsh reality of adult Christmas responsibilities may cause genuine despair, contributing to what is sometimes referred to as the Christmas neurosis.

In the following folk cartoon, the battle of the sexes is set in a Christmas context in which a wife presumably asks her sedentary husband for directions as to what to do with the Christmas tree. His crude metaphorical response, a standard one, namely, "Shove [stick] it up your ass," is taken quite literally by his disgusted spouse. Evidently used to her husband's rude behavior, the wife offers a sarcastic rhetorical question as a rejoinder.

The first version is from Tucson, Arizona, 1987, while the second is from Winnipeg in 1980. For a printed version, see *Maledicta* 8 (1984–85), 14.

" I ASSUME YOU DON'T WANT TO PUT A WREATH ON
THE FRONT DOOR EITHER ! "

"I assume you don't want to put up the outside
lights either."

Never Try to Teach a Pig to Sing

218. These Alimony Payments

Sometimes the battle of the sexes becomes an all-out war whose outcome may be divorce. But even divorce may not end the battle inasmuch as there may be child custody and spousal support disputes. In the following cartoon collected from the lockshop in Dwinelle Hall at the University of California, Berkeley, in 1977, a resentful ex-husband has just personally delivered an alimony payment, perhaps accompanied by a suggestion as to what his former wife should do with it. Once again, the literalization of the earthy metaphor is followed by a sarcastic rejoinder by the wife.

The association of money with the buttocks area is not that uncommon in folklore. The money-feces equation is fairly widespread cross-culturally. Certainly in American culture, one speaks idiomatically of a rich person as having "money up the ass." Also, there are references to being "filthy" rich, and there is a standard folk expression "the day the Eagle shits," referring to payday among federal government employees, including the military.

"YOU REALLY HATE THESE ALIMONY PAYMENTS.... DON'T YOU FRED?"

219. Hand Me the Hair Dryer

Another way out of an unhappy marriage is much more extreme than divorce. It is murder. Domestic violence, sad to say, is much more common than was once thought. The incidence of child abuse and battered wives may or may not be greater now than in the past, but thanks to media coverage and the establishment of organizations offering advice and actual sanctuary, these forms of physical interpersonal violence are widely known by the American public.

In the following folk cartoon, the wife asks for a commonly available appliance, namely, an electric hair dryer, whose shape is vaguely similar to that of a handgun. The first version was collected in Carlisle, Pennsylvania, in 1980, while the second was collected in Chicago in 1983.

"Honey, hand me the hair dryer."

Never Try to Teach a Pig to Sing

"George, hand me the hair dryer."

220. Thirty Reasons Why Cucumbers Are Better than Men

There is probably no more complete list of modern women's complaints about the behavior of men than the list of reasons why cucumbers are better than men, a popular piece of photocopier folklore, which exists in many versions. The text presented below from Los Angeles in 1989 is a relatively short one with only thirty comments. Longer versions include more than one hundred.

The premise is based upon the phallic nature of cucumbers, but the whole thrust of the argument is merely to provide a convenient means of denigrating males. For further discussion of this item, see "97 Reasons Why Cucumbers Are Better than Men," in Alan Dundes, *Cracking Jokes* (Berkeley: Ten Speed Press, 1987), pp. 82–95. Not only is the cucumber list widespread in photocopier tradition, but there are also commercially published versions of it, e.g., Lisa Rahfeldt, *Cucumbers Are Better than Men Because . . .* (Watertown, Mass., 1982), and M. L. Brooks, Donne E. Hanberry, Ivor Matz, Tom Westover, and Craig Westover, *Why Cucumbers Are Better than Men* (New York, 1983). There is also a cleaned up commercial imitation: Herbert I. Kavet, *Teddy Bears Are Better than Men Because . . .* (Watertown, Mass., 1988).

30 REASONS WHY —
CUCUMBERS ARE BETTER THAN MEN BECAUSE:

THE AVERAGE CUCUMBER IS AT LEAST SIX INCHES LONG.

CUCUMBERS STAY HARD FOR A WEEK.

CUCUMBERS DON'T GET TOO EXCITED.

A CUCUMBER NEVER SUFFERS FROM PERFORMANCE ANXIETY.

CUCUMBERS ARE EASY TO PICK-UP.

YOU CAN FONDLE CUCUMBERS IN A SUPERMARKET —
   AND YOU KNOW HOW FIRM IT IS BEFORE YOU TAKE ONE HOME.

A CUCUMBER WILL ALWAYS RESPECT YOU IN THE MORNING.

YOU CAN GO TO A MOVIE WITH A CUCUMBER AND SEE THE MOVIE.

CUCUMBERS DON'T CARE IF YOU'RE A VIRGIN OR NOT.

CUCUMBERS WON'T WRITE YOUR NAME AND NUMBER ON THE MEN'S ROOM WALL.

CUCUMBERS AREN'T INTO ROPE & LEATHER, TALKING DIRTY OR SWINGING
   WITH FRUITS AND NUTS.

YOU CAN HAVE AS MANY CUCUMBERS AS YOU CAN HANDLE.

YOU ONLY EAT CUCUMBERS WHEN YOU FEEL LIKE IT.

CUCUMBERS WON'T ASK ABOUT YOUR LAST LOVER . . .
   OR SPECULATE ABOUT YOUR NEXT ONE.

A CUCUMBER WILL NEVER MAKE A SCENE BECAUSE THERE ARE OTHER CUCUMBERS
   IN THE REFRIGERATOR.

NO MATTER HOW OLD YOU ARE YOU CAN ALWAYS GET A FRESH CUCUMBER.

A CUCUMBER WON'T EAT ALL YOUR FOOD OR DRINK ALL YOUR LIQUOR.

A CUCUMBER DOESN'T FLUSH THE TOILET WHILE YOU'RE TAKING A SHOWER.

WITH A CUCUMBER, THE TOILET SEAT IS ALWAYS THE WAY YOU LEFT IT.

CUCUMBERS WON'T LEAVE DIRTY SHORTS LYING ON THE FLOOR.

CUCUMBERS DON'T COMPARE YOU TO A CENTERFOLD.

CUCUMBERS CAN'T COUNT TO TEN.

YOU ALWAYS KNOW WHERE YOUR CUCUMBER HAS BEEN.

A CUCUMBER WON'T LEAVE YOU FOR A CHEERLEADER OR AN EX-NUN.

YOU WON'T FIND OUT LATER THAT YOUR CUCUMBER . . .
   IS MARRIED.
   LIKES YOU, BUT LOVES YOUR BROTHER.

YOU DON'T HAVE TO WAIT UNTIL HALF-TIME TO TALK TO YOUR CUCUMBER.

CUCUMBERS NEVER EXPECT YOU TO HAVE LITTLE CUCUMBERS.

IT'S EASY TO DROP A CUCUMBER.

A CUCUMBER WILL NEVER CONTEST A DIVORCE, DEMAND A PROPERTY SETTLEMENT
   OR SEEK CUSTODY OF ANYTHING.

NO MATTER HOW YOU SLICE IT, YOU CAN HAVE YOUR CUKE AND EAT IT TOO.

221. Twenty-five Good Reasons Why Beer Is Better than Women

Just as women have their gripes and pet peeves about men, so men have their own list of complaints about women. The device of praising beer as a method of criticizing women may be new. In any event, we have no versions earlier than 1987. If it is a newly created example of photocopier folklore, it may or may not be an attempt to respond to the cucumber agenda ostensibly issued by feminists.

The text was reported from Santa Clara, California, in 1988. For a more extensive litany of male complaints about females, see the discussion of "The Reasons Sheep Are Better than Women" in *Cracking Jokes* (Berkeley: Ten Speed Press, 1987), pp. 89–94.

25 GOOD REASONS
WHY BEER IS BETTER THAN WOMEN

1. YOU CAN ENJOY A BEER ALL MONTH LONG.
2. BEER STAINS WASH OUT.
3. YOU DON'T HAVE TO WINE AND DINE BEER.
4. YOUR BEER WILL ALWAYS WAIT PATIENTLY FOR YOU IN THE CAR WHILE YOU PLAY FOOTBALL.
5. WHEN BEER GOES FLAT, YOU TOSS IT OUT.
6. BEER IS NEVER LATE.
7. A BEER DOESN'T GET JEALOUS WHEN YOU GRAB ANOTHER BEER.
8. HANGOVERS GO AWAY.
9. BEER LABELS COME OFF WITHOUT A FIGHT.
10. WHEN YOU GO TO A BAR, YOU KNOW YOU CAN ALWAYS PICK UP A BEER.
11. BEER NEVER HAS A HEADACHE.
12. YOU DON'T HAVE TO DRIVE A BEER HOME IN THE MORNING.
13. A BEER WON'T GET UPSET IF YOU COME HOME IN THE MORNING.
14. IF YOU POUR A BEER RIGHT, YOU'LL ALWAYS GET GOOD HEAD.
15. A BEER ALWAYS GOES DOWN EASY.
16. YOU CAN HAVE MORE THAN ONE BEER IN A NIGHT AND NOT FEEL GUILTY.
17. YOU CAN SHARE A BEER WITH YOUR FRIENDS.
18. YOU ALWAYS KNOW YOU'RE THE FIRST ONE TO POP A BEER.
19. BEER IS ALWAYS WET.
20. BEER DOESN'T DEMAND EQUALITY.
21. YOU CAN HAVE A BEER IN PUBLIC.
22. A BEER DOESN'T CARE WHEN YOU COME.
23. A FRIGID BEER IS A GOOD BEER.
24. YOU DON'T HAVE TO WASH A BEER BEFORE IT TASTES GOOD.
25. IF YOU CHANGE BEERS YOU DON'T HAVE TO PAY ALIMONY.

222. Anthropological Stages of Man

Life itself can be perceived as a series of developmental stages. One thinks, for example, of Shakespeare's seven ages of man in *As You Like It* (II, vii, 139) in the famous lines which begin "All the world's a stage." In the following mock myth, we find animal names used for sexual punning purposes. This version was reported in Logansport, Indiana, in the late 1960s. (For another version entitled "Ain't It the Truth?" see UFFC-TB, 142.)

ANTHROPOLOGICAL STAGES OF MAN:

IT SEEMS WHEN THE CREATOR WAS MAKING THE WORLD, HE CALLED MAN ASIDE AND BESTOWED UPON HIM TWENTY (20) YEARS OF NORMAL SEX LIFE. MAN WAS HORRIFIED: "ONLY 20 YEARS?" BUT THE CREATOR DIDN'T BUDGE. THAT IS ALL HE WOULD GRANT HIM.

THEN HE CALLED THE MONKEY, AND GAVE HIM 20 YEARS. "BUT I DON'T NEED 20 YEARS," SAID THE MONKEY. "TEN IS PLENTY."

MAN SPOKE UP AND SAID "CAN'T I HAVE THE OTHER 10 YEARS?" THE MONKEY AGREED.

THEN THE CREATOR CALLED THE LION AND GIVE HIM 20 YEARS. THE LION SAID HE ONLY NEEDED 10 YEARS. AGAIN THE MAN ASKED, "CAN'T I HAVE THE OTHER 10 YEARS?" "OF COURSE!" ROARED THE LION.

THEN CAME THE DONKEY. HE WAS GIVEN 20 YEARS AND LIKE THE OTHERS SAID 10 YEARS WAS ALL HE NEEDED. MAN ASKED AGAIN FOR THE 10 YEARS AND AGAIN RECEIVED THEM.

THIS EXPLAINS WHY MAN HAS 20 YEARS OF NORMAL SEX LIFE, 10 YEARS OF MONKEYING AROUND, 10 YEARS OF LION ABOUT IT, AND TEN YEARS OF MAKING AN ASS OF HIMSELF.

---

223. The Geographical Ages of Women

Similar to the "Anthropological Stages of Man" is a series of analogies to continents purportedly describing the sexual appeal of women. There is considerable variation within the common frame of this item as may be seen by comparing the two versions presented below. The first was collected on the West Coast in 1969, while the second was reported in Boston in 1968.

THE GEOGRAPHICAL AGES OF WOMEN

From 15 to 25, she is like
Africa, half virgin, half explored.
From 25 to 35, she is like
Asia, Hot, torrid, and mysterious.
From 35 to 45, she is like
America, Streamlined, efficient,
cooperative.
From 45 to 55, she is like
Europe, Devastated, but still good.
After 55, she is like
Australia, Everyone knows where it is,
but nobody goes there.

Question: Why is a woman like a map of the world?
Because:
Between the ages of 13 and 25 . . . she's like ASIA . . .
Half Virgin and Half Explored!
Between 25 and 35 . . . She's like AFRICA . . .
Hot and Mysterious!
Between 35 and 45 . . . She's like America . . .
Cool, Calculating and Commercial!
Between 45 and 65 . . . Like Europe . . .
Devastated . . . But still some Interesting Spots!
After 65 . . . Like Iceland . . . Everyone knows
where it is
But who the hell wants to go there!

In a similar version collected in Washington, D.C., in 1976, we find such variations as "From 36 to 46 she is like the U.S.A., generous with her resources. From 46 to 59 she is like the lost continent, waiting to be discovered." For earlier versions in print, see *Over Sexteen* (New York: Elgart, 1951), p. 26; Harold H. Hart, ed.,

The Complete Immortalia (New York: Bell Publishing Company, 1971), p. 458; Andrew L. Cleveland, *Dirty Stories for All Occasions* (New York: Galahad Books, 1980), p. 63. For a Swedish version, see MF, 79; for a version from England, see RJ, 92.

224. Sales Tax

The connection between government and sex is a longstanding one. Scandals in various governments are revealed from time to time. In this card collected in Washington, D.C. (as well as in others collected in California), the woman as sex object strikes back by couching the acts of government in carnal terms. Legman cites several versions, e.g., one from Washington, D.C., in 1951 and another from Nice, France, in 1974. He indicates that the item goes back at least to the 1930s and usually is told with the president of the United States as the central figure. See RDJ, 254 and NLM, 227, 746. For other versions, see Maude Thickett, *Outrageously Offensive Jokes II* (New York: Pocket Books, 1984), pp. 18–19; Blanche Knott, *Truly Tasteless Jokes VII* (New York: St. Martin's Press, 1987), p. 71.

SALES TAX -- SALES TAX

The Governor went around the State to get 3 beautiful girls, a red head, blonde and a brunette. To the red head he said, "I am the Governor, how much will it cost me to have intercourse with you?" She said $100.00. To the blonde he said the same, she said $200.00. To the brunette he said the same. She smartly replied, "If you can raise my skirt as high as Taxes and get my panties as low as wages are, and get that thing of yours as hard as times are and screw me like you do the public, it won't cost you a damn cent.

Never Try to Teach a Pig to Sing

225. Women's Lib Motto

While ideally in marriage decisions should be jointly made by both husband and wife, the fact is that one or another in a given family may assume the role of key decision maker. A conventional folk idiom referring to family dominance asks "Who wears the pants?" with the implication being that men are expected to fill that role. Presumably men wear pants while women wear dresses. However, in those families where it is obvious to all concerned that the woman is in charge, not the man, it might very well be said of that woman that "she wears the pants" in the family.

In the following item, there is an interesting play on the pants metaphor. Also, the woman is forced to use her sexuality or the denial of it as a weapon in order to prevail. The text was recorded in Carlisle, Pennsylvania, in 1980. For other versions, see UFFC-TB, 143; Shelli Sonstein, *The Thoroughly Tasteful Dirty Joke Book* (New York: Stein and Day, 1985), p. 86; Blanche Knott, *Truly Tasteless Jokes V* (New York: St. Martin's Press, 1985), pp. 54–55; and Julius Alvin, *Doubly Gross Jokes*, Vol. V (New York: Zebra Books, 1986), p. 128. For an English version, see TCB, 154.

Womens' Lib Motto

A young couple just married were in their honeymoon suite on their wedding night. As they undressed for bed the husband who was a big burly bruiser, tossed his pants to his bride and said, "Here put these on." She put them on and the waist was twice the size of her body. "I can't wear your pants!" she said. "That's right!" said the husband, "and don't you forget it. I'm the man who wears the pants in this family!" With that she flipped him her panties and said, "Try these on." He tried them on and found he could only get them on as far as his knee cap. He said, "Hell I can't get into your pants!" She said "That's right' and that's the way it's going to be until your goddamn attitude changes!"

Never Try to Teach a Pig to Sing

226. The Missing Key

Women did not always control their own bodies. It is one thing for a woman to announce to her man that he will not get into her pants. It is quite another for her to be locked in a chastity belt where she does not possess the key. In the following cartoon collected in Washington, D.C., in 1970, a knight appears unable to open the lock of a fair maiden's chastity belt. The sexual symbolism of male keys fitting into female locks seems well attested in this instance and in folklore generally. For a representative discussion of the chastity belt, see Taylor Hemingway, *Sex Control: Curious Customs of Medieval Times* (Harriman, Tennessee: Pioneer Press, 1953).

For the standard joke in which a knight leaving for the crusades entrusts his best friend with the key to his wife's chastity belt and after being on the road for only a few minutes is overtaken by his friend who exclaims, "You gave me the wrong key," see *Sextra Special* (New York: Scylla, 1953), p. [61]. There is yet another common joke in oral tradition set in Arthurian times in which Merlin designs a special guillotine-like chastity belt mechanism to protect Guinevere. Arthur rides off to slay dragons and upon his return, he conducts a "short-arm" inspection of all the knights of the Round Table and discovers that the *membrum virile* of every one of them was nicked or cut except for that of Sir Lancelot. Arthur praises Lancelot for upholding the honor of the Round Table and offers him anything in the kingdom he might desire. Lancelot has only to name it, but Lancelot is not able to speak. For representative texts of this joke, see *Playboy's Party Jokes 4* (Chicago: PBJ Books, 1970), p. 185; Julius Alvin, *Gross Jokes* (New York: Zebra Books, 1983), p. 98; Blanche Knott, *Truly Tasteless Jokes IV* (New York: Pinnacle Books, 1984), p. 69.

Never Try to Teach a Pig to Sing

227. You Think You Have Problems!

Another metaphor for sexuality analogous to the key and the lock consists of an electrical plug and socket. The metaphor is explicit insofar as one can refer to the plug as male and the receptacle or socket as female.

The problem of matching plugs and sockets is a real one. Modern electrical appliances often have three prongs, one of which is a ground. These plugs do not fit into old-fashioned conventional sockets which can accommodate only the two-prong plugs. In such instances, one needs an adaptor to bridge the gap.

In the following cartoon from a Pacific Gas and Electric office in San Francisco in November of 1989, it is of interest that it is the male robot who has the old-fashioned plug that will not fit into the newer three-slotted receptacle of the female robot. There may also be an implicit hint that purely mechanical sex can also be frustrating.

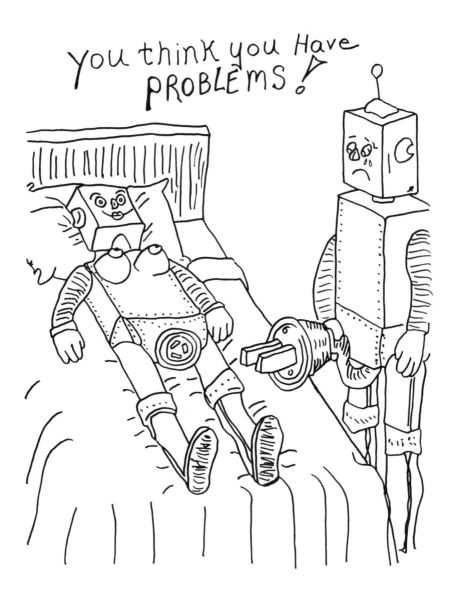

Never Try to Teach a Pig to Sing

228. Poor Joe

There may be any number of reasons why sexual union does not occur. In the following exchange between husband and wife, we find an unusual use of a circus metaphor as a code for them to communicate without revealing the covert message to their small child. There are a large number of traditional euphemisms employed by women to refer to menstruation. See Janice Delaney, Mary Jane Lupton, and Emily Toth, *The Curse: A Cultural History of Menstruation* (New York: Mentor, 1977).

The text was collected in Castro Valley, California, in 1973. For another version, entitled "Show Off," see *Furthermore Over Sexteen*, Vol. 4 (New York: Grayson, 1956), p. 106.

Poor Joe

Joe woke up one morning and looked for his wife, but his wife wasn't there. She had awakened and was preparing breakfast in the kitchen. Joe was afraid he might spoil things by getting up, so he called his little boy and sent this note to his wife:

THE TENT POLE IS UP,
THE CANVAS IS SPREAD,
THE HELL WITH BREAKFAST,
COME BACK TO BED.

The wife answered the note and sent it back by the boy. It read:

TAKE THE TENT POLE DOWN,
PUT THE CANVAS AWAY,
THE MONKEY HAD A HEMORRHAGE,—
NO CIRCUS TODAY.

229. I Do So Enjoy Sex!!

The idea that a sexual act can be consummated in a matter of minutes surely reflects a male rather than a female aesthetic. A common complaint among women is that men are too often of the "slam [or wham] bam, thank you ma'am" school. According to this school, the men take their pleasure quickly with little or no thought to the needs or desires of the women. Jokes about the supposed disparity between male and female sexual appetites abound. Typically the male is oversexed while the female is undersexed. The following folk cartoon makes fun of both these stereotypes. This version was collected in Concord, New Hampshire, in 1977.

For another text (without a cartoon), see *Playboy's Party Jokes 4* (Chicago: PBJ Books, 1970), p. 181. It should be noted that sometimes it is the female, not the male, who desires more sexual activity. For example, in one joke a couple with marital problems goes to a marriage counselor. The husband complains that his wife doesn't prepare proper meals for him, while the wife's grievance is that the husband does not fulfill his conjugal responsibilities. The counselor offers a solution: the wife will attend cooking school, while the husband is to sleep with his wife semi-annually. Leaving the counselor's office, the wife takes her husband by the hand and asks, "Tell me, how many times a week is semi-annually?" Of course, this joke does portray the wife as being stereotypically dumb. See Andrew L. Cleveland, *Dirty Stories for All Occasions* (New York: Galahad Books, 1980), p. 100.

"I do so enjoy sex!! But this sex fiend expects it two or three times a year."

230. For Our Retirement?

Sometimes the stereotypes can be reversed. In the following cartoon collected in Berkeley in the 1980s, it is the woman who is interested in sex and the man who is unable to perform.

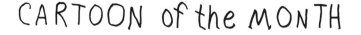

CARTOON of the MONTH

MY GOD DIDN'T YOU SAVE ANYTHING FOR OUR RETIREMENT?

231. Once More for Old Time's Sake

The familiar theme of the supposed lack of sexuality among the elderly forms the subject of the following folk cartoon. In the cartoon, not only are elderly males potent, but elderly females are depicted as being fertile. We shall present three versions to demonstrate the substantial variation of this item. The first version was collected in San Francisco in 1969; the second in Wabash, Indiana, also in 1969; while the third is from a San Francisco office of Pacific Gas and Electric in 1976.

The differences in the settings (as indicated, for example, by the clothing styles and chair designs) suggest that the stereotypic theme applies equally to the humble and the rich. Noteworthy in the third version is the apparent portrait of a pig (presumably of the male chauvinist variety) which hangs over the male figure. The chauvinism is also implicit in the caption insofar as a male's moment of pleasure results in the burden of pregnancy for the female.

"YOU AND YOUR ONCE MORE FOR OLD TIME'S SAKE"

Never Try to Teach a Pig to Sing

"You—and your once more for old time's sake!"

232. Women's Faults Are Many

While in theory it might be possible to be pro-female without being anti-male, in practice it is much easier to feel superior at the expense of some other group which is deemed inferior. So it should come as no real surprise to learn that the feminist movement has spawned some anti-male folklore. The following pronouncement begins with feigned humility on the part of women, but ends by humbling men. It was collected in Dublin, California, in 1977. For an English version, see YWIW, [105].

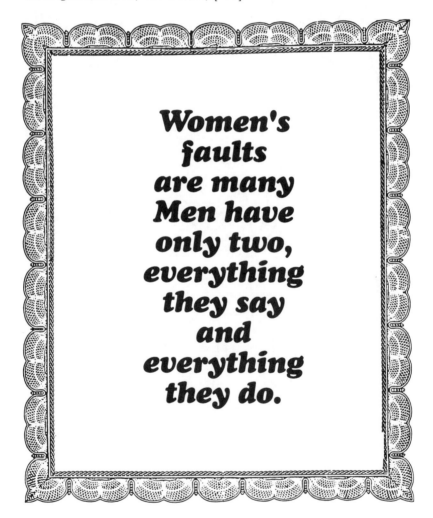

Women's faults are many Men have only two, everything they say and everything they do.

233. What's Going On?

There is a proverbial expression in the United States to the effect that "Behind every great man there stands a woman." A modern parody no doubt inspired by the feminist movement adds, "Who says he's not" to the adage. It is often true that men nominally in charge get credit for work carried out by female subordinates. Some women who are administrative assistants or executive secretaries feel this quite keenly. It is they who are close to the day-to-day operation of the office, they feel, not the boss. This is the subject of the following item collected from a female employee of a trucking company in Eureka, California, in November 1989.

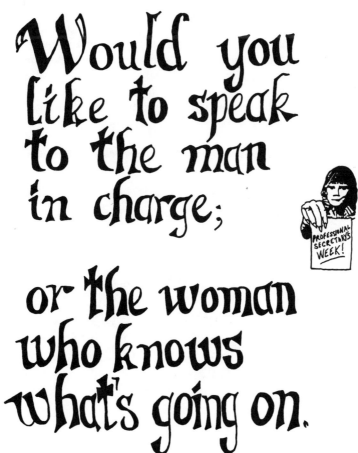

Would you like to speak to the man in charge; or the woman who knows what's going on.

234. Twice as Much as a Man

In folklore, it is part of convention that young men slay dragons (cf. Aarne-Thompson tale type 300, "The Dragon-Slayer," where the hero rescues the princess). In the modern world, women in order to compete with men on an equal basis have to slay dragons too. But to succeed, women feel they have to perform at a higher level than men.

In the following folk cartoon from San Carlos, California, in 1975, we can see this principle at work. The cartoon was collected from a female informant who was working as a tile layer in construction, normally a male occupation. Most versions have the text only, without the dragon-killing drawing. It should also be pointed out that the heroine in the cartoon uses male symbols. Moreover, her sword is bigger than the man's; her helmet's horns appear larger than those on the man's helmet. Her sword is piercing the dragon while the man's is sheathed. Certainly her dragon dwarfs the puny little dragon the male warrior is holding by its tail. Finally, it should also be remembered that dragons are typically male, which means that the heroine has thoroughly conquered a male antagonist. For another version, see RJ, 76.

A woman has to do twice as much as a man in order to be considered half as good.

Fortunately, that isn't too difficult.

235. Final Masterpiece

Much has been written about the Bible's male patriarchal bias. Adam is created before Eve — at least in the version of the creation of man in which Eve is molded from Adam's rib. A male Noah builds an ark to save mankind and the animal world while Mrs. Noah doesn't even rate having a name. In the New Testament, Jesus, a male, is said to be the son of a male God. The Holy Trinity consists of three male beings: the Father, the Son, and the Holy Ghost. To the extent that the Bible continues to serve as a charter for worldview in Western culture, the role of women remains that of second-class citizen. Adam's rib doesn't jibe with women's lib!

While the world has changed dramatically over the past two millennia, the Bible basically has not. Only the interpretation of the Bible can change over time. The text of the Bible remains fixed, reflecting a historical time and place and more importantly a worldview vastly different from contemporary society.

We choose to end this volume with a folk attempt to re-interpret the biblical creation story in Genesis because we believe it shows the endless vitality of folklore and its incredible ability to adapt to new situations and new values. Just as in "The Evolution of Authority" (item 187 above), man is but a stage before women's ultimate dominance. So the creation of mankind in Genesis can be seen in the same light. For an English version, see OHB, 50.

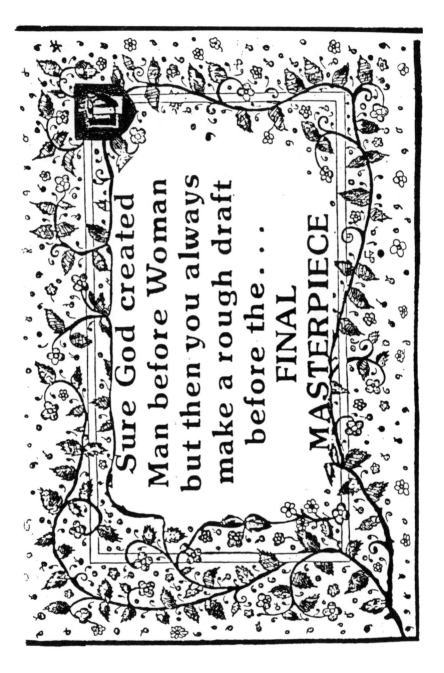

Sure God created Man before Woman but then you always make a rough draft before the . . . . FINAL MASTERPIECE

Conclusions

From our studies of photocopier folklore over the past twenty-five years and from the content of this volume, we feel secure in saying that this form of urban folklore continues to flourish both in terms of quantity and quality. Whereas some folklorists tend to feel that they are salvaging the last remnants of a fading ballad tradition or a dying local custom, we feel fortunate to be investigating a lively and burgeoning phenomenon. There seems to us to be more and more photocopier folklore circulating—not only in the United States, but abroad as well, judging from the appearance of collections published in other countries. All indications are that as photocopiers become more and more common around the world, photocopier folklore will proliferate accordingly. If we are correct, then we believe our several attempts to document this fascinating modern tradition may prove of use to future students of what is likely to become a worldwide tradition.

We understand that students of high culture may well regard the contents of this volume as trivial ephemera. Our position is that this is precisely why it is so valuable. It is what is common to a people which defines that people and is therefore especially worthy of both preservation and analysis. Nothing is so trivial that it cannot yield important insights into the people's minds who create, transmit, and above all, enjoy it. The fact that some of the photocopier folklore leads a precarious existence, moving as it does from one bulletin board to another, only underscores the necessity for recording these materials in a rigorous way. It is our impression that similar materials may have flourished through print shops in centuries past, but they were not systematically collected. Even now, the majority of university and college libraries do not make any concerted effort to collect the kinds of photocopier folklore included in this volume.

Virtually all of the major themes and anxieties of contemporary American culture are to be found throughout this collection. Samples of these themes would include alienation, bureaucracy, dieting, ethnic stereotypes, feminism, job security, racism, retirement, sexism, stress, technological change, and women's liberation, among others.

The picture of American life which emerges from a reading of these materials is a complex one, full of anxieties about one's job, one's interpersonal relations (including sexual ones), and one's future. Yet it should be kept in mind that the picture presented is one painted by the American people themselves. We did not invent any of the items contained in this volume. All of the items, to the best of our knowledge, are currently circulating from office to office, from individual to individual. If anyone is offended by some of the materials, that is to be expected. Folklore is almost always concerned with the "cutting edge" of serious issues. When something cuts, it can hurt. What the reader should keep in mind is that the materials we have presented are a reflection of American society as it is. If an item is racist or sexist, that is because the society which produced it is racist or sexist. One should not blame the mirror for the image or similarly the messenger who brings the bad news. The only materials we have consciously omitted are extreme forms of sexually explicit traditions.

Besides the scholarly value of the materials here assembled, we would like to express our hope that the general reader will find many individual items he or she can enjoy. We ourselves must confess that we continue to be vastly amused by many of the items even though we have seen numerous versions of them over an extended period of time. The quality of folk creativity is often demeaned by elitists, but we feel just the opposite. If an item is clever enough to survive and circulate, it must have some element of worth, some modicum of appeal to the psyches of those who transmit it. In folklore, if an item has passed the test of time, that in itself says something about its value. No one would bother to pass on an item of photocopier folklore if he or she did not find it meaningful in some way.

One should not be fooled or misled by the humor of some of the items. Humor typically masks only what is most serious in life. The greater the humor, the more important the subject matter. If American folk humor can provide a useful window into American culture, then this volume should offer a number of novel views. Of course, not all of the items are humorous. Some of the folk poetry inclines more toward nostalgia and sentiment. Here the tone is more of sadness and regret, not humor. But whether amusing or philosophical, *all* the items are authentic pieces of Americana.

We look forward with great anticipation to the continuing evolution of photocopier folklore. We have no doubt whatsoever that hundreds of new items will be created by new generations of office workers and others. These new creations, if they effectively encapsulate an issue of concern in a sufficiently witty and appealing fashion, will no doubt join the hundreds upon hundreds of photocopier items already in tradition.

Eventually there should be extended in-depth analyses of individual specimens of photocopier folklore, just as there have been monographs devoted to the study of individual ballads or folktales. In a volume like this, we are limited as to how much we can say about any one item and the number of versions or variants of that item we can reasonably present. But each of the items contained in this volume represents a separate challenge to the serious folklore researcher. And there are other research possibilities. Rhetorical techniques could be explored, e.g., the literalization of metaphor (from folk speech) as the basis for cartoons. The particular animals chosen as vehicles for photocopier folklore would make a fascinating project to investigate. The borrowing of selected popular culture characters, e.g., from comic strips, for the photocopier tradition would be yet another interesting topic to probe and explain.

Our goal in this volume was to continue our efforts to sample and document one of the most exciting and important strands of modern American folklore. Most of the materials contained in this volume are not discussed by American folklore scholars and are not to be found in the standard anthologies of American folklore. If our collection of photocopier folklore at the same time brings laughter and pleasure to readers not concerned with the scientific value of this neglected form of contemporary folklore, so much the better. Knowledge and data don't have to be boring and dull. So it is our sincere hope that the readers will have enjoyed this substantial sampling of photocopier folklore as much as we have enjoyed collecting it and making it available for publication.

Books in the Humor in Life and Letters Series